Get Your Share

Get Your Share

The Everyday Woman's Guide to Striking It Rich in the Stock Market

Julie Stav
with Deborah Adamson

B BERKLEY BOOKS, NEW YORK

This book is an original publication of The Berkley Publishing Group.

GET YOUR SHARE

A Berkley Book
Published by The Berkley Publishing Group,
a division of Penguin Putnam Inc.,
375 Hudson Street
New York, New York 10014.

The Penguin Putnam Inc. World Wide Web site address is
http://www.penguinputnam.com

Berkley hardcover edition: April 2000

Library of Congress Cataloguing-in-Publication Data

Stav, Julie.
    Get your share : the everyday woman's guide to striking it rich in the stock market / by Julie Stav with Deborah Adamson.
    p. cm.
    ISBN: 0-425-17392-5
    1. Stocks.   2. Investments.   I. Adamson, Deborah.   II. Title.
    HG4661.S75 2000
    332.63'22—dc21   99-054276

BERKLEY®
Berkley Books are published by The Berkley Publishing Group,
a division of Penguin Putnam Inc.,
375 Hudson Street, New York, New York 10014.
BERKLEY and the "B" design
are trademarks belonging to Penguin Putnam Inc.

PRINTED IN THE UNITED STATES OF AMERICA

10 9 8 7 6

*To my dad, who taught me early in life
that having class has nothing to do
with having money.*

ACKNOWLEDGMENTS

My most sincere thanks to my children, Tony and Jonathan, who temporarily lost their cook, housekeeper, psychologist and nurse. To my husband, Danny, who stood by my side regardless of the personality I happened to wear at the time.

To my writer, Deborah, whose gift of expression helped me put my dreams into words. To our editor, Chris Parker, who polished our words into a clean shine.

To Chuck Hurewitz, my attorney, friend and trusted mentor, who believed in my message from the beginning.

To Harvey Klinger, my book agent, who took a chance with a novice.

To Denise, Leslie, Hillary, Lisa, and Martha at Penguin Putnam, whose energy and nurturing filled me with confidence and determination. Thanks to all!

CONTENTS

Born to Be Wild
(Even on a Busy Schedule)

By picking up this book, you've taken a big step toward securing your financial future. Sure, you're busy. You may have a crying baby on one arm, a load of laundry waiting to be washed, and a house that would drive Martha Stewart to tears. Time for a book? Let alone an *investment* book?

Let me put it this way. If you've been yearning to learn about the stock market but cringed at the thought of burying your nose in a boring textbook, set your worries aside. We're going to have fun and you will still discover the secrets of making money in the stock market. We'll go through the basics of investing together, hand in hand. I promise to explain financial concepts in plain English. By the time you finish the last chapter, you will have discovered a whole new person that you never knew existed before: the wild, Wall Street woman in you!

Ha! you say. The closest thing you ever get to wild these days is when you dust off that leopard-print blouse that's been sitting in your closet since high school. But it happens all the time. In my twenty years of financial planning experience, I've seen thousands of women go wild about the stock market once they've learned how to invest. They found making money exhilarating. These women already were Mommy Maries and Career Carries. But now they've added one more persona: Wall Street Winnie.

All I did was give them a taste of the stock market, the tools to navigate financial waters, and the confidence to stick with investing—and boy, have they surged ahead like a pack of screaming women who've just spotted a half-off sale at Macy's! They became excited because a whole new world was revealed to them, a universe they never saw before. In a way, they reminded me of my first-grade students when I was a schoolteacher. After I taught the kids how to read, their eyes were opened in awe at the wondrous world that unfolded before them.

Today, I may be a financial planner but in my heart I'm still a teacher. Let me show you how to walk in the ways of investing, and when you've mastered the basics, you can take off running! I've always believed that the mark of a good teacher is made by the number of students that surpass her. But first, you'll need a place to start. This book will give you the basic knowledge to begin developing your own investment strategy. It will help you build a good foundation upon which you'll eventually develop your own style. After all, there isn't one foolproof investment approach that works all the time; if there were, we wouldn't see all those investment books in the store. In truth, most investors end up blending various methods to create one that suits them.

For my strategy, the key to success is as simple as this: Date your stocks, don't marry them. Try them out but don't hesitate to say, "Thanks for a great evening, good night," to those that don't cut it. In investing, as in dating, you need to keep your standards high—and I'll show you how. Once you find those great stocks, you can make a killing!

Make Your Life a Real Gem, Not Cubic Zirconia

It's about time women learned to be financially independent. We love our men, but they won't be around forever. Did you know that nine out of ten women will end up having to take care of themselves? That's due to divorce, widowhood (we outlive men by an average of seven years), or staying single by choice. Whether we like it or not, we'll have to take care of ourselves at one time or another. A secure financial future goes beyond working for a living. We need to know how to save and, more important, invest the money we earn so we can buy a house, pay for our children's college tuition, and still have enough left over for a cushy retirement. Did you know that a sixty-five-old retiree today who is expected to live for another twenty years will need at least $300,000 to live modestly? If you're planning to go on Caribbean cruises every year, you'll need to retire with even more money.

Even if you're blessed with a plush inheritance, it's still important to be in control of your finances. You want to be in charge of it so you won't have to depend on other people's advice—which may be wrong, and you'll end up paying the consequences. Yes, even investment professionals in their nice, shiny offices can make mistakes. It happens all the time.

The bottom line *is* the bottom line. We may not want to deal with money issues now, but we simply must. Sure, money doesn't buy happiness, but it gives us security, freedom, and power.

Investing in the stock market is a way you can start securing your future now. Don't worry, it's not hard to do. Wall Street might look scary, but it doesn't have to be. The key is to invest well. I'll teach you how to buy and sell stocks, read technical charts as easily as you would a mail-order catalog, *and* we'll still have a ball. Follow along and I'll share the secrets of investment mavens with you. Even if you start out without a clue—"What's a stock? What's the Dow?"—stick around and I promise you'll sound and act like a pro when we're done.

Women and Men Come from Different Planets

First, let's agree on one thing: We're women and we see life— and investing—differently from men. Women really *are* from Venus and men are from Mars even in the way we approach our finances. But it's okay to be ourselves. We don't have to act like our husbands, boyfriends, fathers, or sons. In fact, in investing, it's better that we don't. According to the National Association of Investors Corp., women-only investment clubs have earned an average of 21 percent on their money each year since their groups started, compared with 15 percent for men.

That's because women tend to be better researchers, taking time to evaluate stocks before buying or selling. Ironically, a woman's perceived weakness is also a strength in disguise: Women are less confident about their stock-picking abilities than men, so we aren't as hasty about making our investment decisions. A man's overconfidence leads to an inflated sense of his abilities and translates into a lagging performance, according to a study by two professors at the University of California, Davis.

So women are inherently good investors, given a chance to learn. You don't even have to be as rich as Oprah to start. If you join an investment club or buy shares in a mutual fund, you can begin investing with as little as $10 to $50 a month. *You can do it;* thousands of women across America invest successfully every year.

Even so, one of a woman's biggest obstacles to success is self-doubt. We tend to underestimate our own abilities. But let's not confuse lack of knowledge with lack of intelligence. It's true that most of us are not especially exposed to investments, but I'll help you catch up. One of these days you'll astonish family or friends at dinner with your financial know-how: "Please pass the butter . . . Did you see the earnings of Children's Place today? Beat analysts' estimates . . . No, thank you, I don't want more corn. Billy, stop picking at your food."

Don't Just Give Us Directions, Show Us How to Read a Map

Women tend to be successful students of investing because we are not afraid to say "I don't know" or "I'm lost." Men, however, usually don't like to admit that they need help. Remember the times when your husband or date would drive aimlessly around a neighborhood but refuse to ask for directions? When your cries of "why don't you just ask someone" went unheeded? Fortunately, women tend not to be that way. In investing, as in life, it's a virtue to have the courage to admit that you're lost or you don't understand. That's how you learn. At times, you may even be pleasantly surprised that the answer is one that you know after all. Research shows that we women understand more than we give ourselves credit for.

Just remember, knowledge is power. It's your blood-sweat-

and-tears money that's at stake here. You want to make sure you know how to invest your savings—or at least understand how others are handling your money. You won't regret it.

Now let's start the adventure. It's time to get wild.

CHAPTER ONE

I Hate Math . . . But
I Love Profits!

It's been twenty years since you graduated from high school, but you still have the same nightmare: The clock ticks five minutes before the bell. With clammy hands, you nervously pore over the last few questions on the math final. Your throat is dry and your poor stomach is doing the samba. Hoping for the best, you scribble down some answers in a hurry. It's your last exam as a senior in high school and you wish never to see another math equation in your life again. *Brring!* You wake up in a cold sweat.

Today, you're a confident businesswoman who tries her best to balance the demands of family and career. The insecure teen is gone forever, replaced by a woman with her own sense of style. You've learned a lot over the years, lessons you wouldn't give up to be a teenager again. But there's one thing that hasn't changed: your feelings about numbers. You realize that whether you're eighteen, thirty-eight, or fifty-eight, you like math about as much as you like an IRS audit.

It's only natural that you're tiptoeing around the idea of investing today. Sure, you'd rather be chained and flogged than spend an hour with an algebra book. But guess what? *You don't have to be a math whiz to invest.* Can you add and subtract? Multiply and divide? Great. That's all the math you need. Better yet, get a calculator and you won't even need to do all that. With a "sure can!" attitude and a finger to punch in numbers, you're all set.

Still not convinced? Get a cup of coffee and let's talk.

"But I'm Not Rich! I Don't Have Money to Invest."

Do you have $25 a month? That's less than $1 a day and about the cost of two Starbucks café mochas a week. With your coffee money, you can start investing in a mutual fund. What's a mutual fund? Imagine that investors from all over the world send money to an investment company. This money is collected and put in a "basket" called a mutual fund. A manager is hired to handle the money in the basket. He or she can invest it in different ways— some conservative, some on the wild side. In America, we can choose from more than 10,000 different funds. Like Baskin-Robbins, there's a flavor to satisfy every craving.

We'll talk more about mutual funds in Chapter 8.

Another way to invest with a small amount is through an investment club. This is a group whose members gather regularly to educate themselves and socialize. Together, you'll decide which companies to buy into with money collected from each person— and you can start with as little as $10 a month. That might not sound like much, but if twenty-five women pooled their money for six months, you're talking $1,500! That's serious money.

An investment club of like-minded people can be a fun and nurturing experience. There will be a dozen or so other would-be investors in the club who will learn about stocks right along with you. Together, through hard work and humor, you'll figure it out. One way to set the right mood is to use puns for a club name: One group called themselves "Cents and Sensibility" since they're Jane Austen fans. Another club of golden-haired gals came up with "Stocks and Blondes."

I think investment clubs were created with women in mind. Like geese, we tend to flock. Have you ever seen men at a dinner table suddenly get up as a group and say, "We're going to the men's room; we'll be right back." Never. It's the women who go there together. Why? Who knows? At least you'll have someone with you who'll sound an alert if you tuck the back of your skirt into your panty hose.

We'll get into investment clubs in Chapter 9.

If you're not the group type and would rather invest by yourself, that's fine too. Maybe you've been itching to get a better return on your savings account or CD (certificate of deposit). Perhaps you just want to make more money from your secret stash. "What stash?" you ask innocently. Come on, I know many of you have a little "rainy day" money secretly tucked away somewhere—in an old mayonnaise jar, perhaps? Let's take all that money and run . . . to more profitable investments you'll pick out with the knowledge I'll share with you in the next few chapters.

"I Don't Have Time to Invest!"

You have more time than you think. Aren't you the person who would drag your boyfriend to at least six shoe stores in the mall before buying a pair of black pumps? If you can spend hours scouting for the best shoe deal, why not take the time to look for the best investment so you can make money? That way, you'll be able to afford as many shoes as you want.

If you'd rather hire your own financial advisor, make sure that you understand something about investing. Otherwise, you'll be blindly handing over control of your hard-earned dollars to someone else—and how will you know if he or she is doing a good job? When you understand investment basics, you can better monitor the advisor's actions by asking the right questions.

It's just like cleaning your house. No one can clean your house as well as you can because you know best what areas need the most work. If you don't have time to Hoover, Spic and Span, and Lysol your home, you can hire a maid service. But without your help, the maid won't do a good job because only you know the trouble spots. The best solution is for both of you to work together: Tell the maid the areas that need the hardest scrubbing and let him or her do the job. With an investment advisor, it's the same thing: Work together to achieve your financial goals. But you can only collaborate successfully if you: 1) communicate your needs, expectations, and risk tolerance, and 2) understand what he or she is doing.

"My Husband Takes Care of Investing."

I'm glad that your husband is the family's financial cowboy. It's wonderful he's shouldering this responsibility. But that doesn't mean you shouldn't have a hand in running the ranch as well. For one, you'll likely have to fend for yourself someday and thus will need to learn how to manage money. According to the U.S. Census Bureau, 40 percent of women who are sixty-five years or older live alone. By the time women reach or go past the age of eighty-five, half of them will be single. Also, you might be pleasantly surprised to find out that your husband welcomes and appreciates your interest. I've had men tell me so.

Let me tell you about Vicki. Like many women, she had left the family's investments in her husband's capable hands for most of her life. She was content to run the household and take care of the children. When her husband died, the sixty-five-year-old housewife suddenly had to take over his duties, and that included managing their investments. She panicked. Vicki was Mom and Grandma, not Donald Trump! Sure, she could handle the household budget. But stocks and bonds? It seemed impossible.

So she did what seemed like the next best thing: She handed over her money to another man—her bank's investment advisor. For six months she bought whatever mutual fund he recommended, no questions asked. It was at this point in her life that she came to one of my seminars. Vicki learned about stocks and bonds and how they fit into her financial future. As her eyes were opened, it was exciting to see this knowledge transform her from a fragile caterpillar into a magnificent butterfly that flew high!

One day she went to see the bank representative armed with this newfound knowledge. When Vicki began to ask questions about the mutual fund he was pushing—after all, she needed to check if it was an appropriate investment for her—he seemed annoyed and insulted that she questioned his authority! She broke the easy pattern he was used to: Tell this lady what to buy, she'll write a check, and he can go home with another commission. *How dare she ask questions about her money?* But Vicki had a big smile on her face. For the first time since her husband died, she understood what was going on.

Sure, her bank had played an important role in her life, providing federally insured savings and checking accounts. But Vicki realized that it was not necessarily the best place for her investments. *Stocks and mutual funds bought from the bank are not safer than getting them elsewhere: They're neither insured nor guaranteed.* The next time I saw Vicki, she was a new woman, blossoming in her sixties. "Julie," she breathed. "I feel wonderful!" Guess what? She's a confident and successful investor today. As a member of two investment clubs—one of which she presides over as an officer—Vicki has switched from being controlled to being in control of her money.

"I Already Save Money!"

You are way ahead of most people if you're an avid saver. But are you saving smart? "I put my money in a bank CD earning 5 percent," you say. "It's safe." Not exactly. I'm not saying that thieves will break in and take your money—they might, but then again the government insures the funds. I'm talking about getting mugged by the sneakiest robber of all: inflation.

Every year, the prices of food, clothing, shelter, and transportation go up. A burger that cost you fifty cents in high school might cost $1.99 today. That's inflation—the gradual creeping up of prices over time. The interest you're earning in the bank has to grow much faster than inflation for you not only to keep up with increases in costs, but to have plenty left over for those extras that make life more enjoyable and colorful.

Investing your money in stocks can yield much greater riches. It beats savings accounts, government and good-quality corporate bonds, money market accounts, and bank CDs.

Let's imagine that Mrs. Johnson put $1,000 in a savings account in 1926 that paid 3.7 percent interest a year. The bank looked like a safe place for her money. The teller was pleasant, the lobby looked elegant, and she was reassured by the impressive building; it symbolized stability. It made her feel safe to open an account there. By 1998, she's had time to have children, grandchildren, and great-grandchildren, and she decided to pull the money out of Rock Solid Savings Bank. Her balance would be about $14,000. That doesn't sound shabby, right?

But how much could that $14,000 buy in 1998? Look at it this way: In 1926, $1,000 could buy her almost three brand-new Model T Fords. But in 1998, after almost a century, her money only earned enough to buy a Ford Escort! Talk about erosion of her purchasing power. Rising prices have won this round.

Now turn back the clock. What if Mrs. Johnson couldn't make it to the bank that day in 1926? Instead, she stayed home and heard her husband talk about government savings bonds. They paid 5.33 percent interest a year and so she put her $1,000 there. Seventy-two years later her money had grown to more than $42,000. That's better. She could buy two Saturns today and still have a little money left over.

How would life have been different for Mrs. Johnson if she invested in the stock market? By putting $1,000 in large-company stocks, her money would have risen to $2.1 million by 1998—and that takes into account the stock market crash of 1929. If Mrs. Johnson invested in small-company stocks, by 1998 she would have had over $4 million! She could pay cash for a fleet of Mercedes-Benzes, paint them every color of the rainbow, and park them in a special garage at her mansion in Palm Springs.

"Okay, I'm In. What Do I Have to Do?"

Read and learn. In the next few chapters, we'll take an easy stroll down Wall Street, arm in arm. We'll walk, not sprint, through our lessons because we want to know them well.

We'll need a few tools to help us: *The Wall Street Journal*, access to Value Line stock reports and Morningstar mutual fund reports at the public library, a calculator, and pencil and paper. If you're hooked up to the Internet, you can find a treasure trove of free financial information at the touch of a button. Ask your local library if they offer Internet access and classes.

But the most important friend you'll need is commitment. You have to be committed to this endeavor for it to work. It doesn't mean that you'll always have time to do research. You won't, and that's okay. Let's face it, most of us lead busy lives. But I want your promise that you won't let this information go to waste because it's critically important.

Learning how to invest well spells the difference between retiring on a tight budget and financial freedom in your golden years so you can live comfortably and pursue hobbies you never had time for before. Maybe you can finally take that oil-painting class or learn how to cook French cuisine—in Paris! Wouldn't life be richer? Whatever you decide to do, at least you can rest assured that you'll be able to afford it.

So get ready—it's time to learn and earn!

CHAPTER TWO

What's a Stock Anyway?

It's another busy Saturday. The hustle and bustle at home reminds you of New York's Grand Central Station at rush hour: The dogs are barking; they want their food. Your husband's calling, he can't find his favorite golf shirt. The television is on full blast, ignored by your boys, who are wrestling on the floor. Your teen, Katie, is chattering away on the phone to her boyfriend while she paints her nails blue. As for you, there's a list of chores to do. In the back of your mind, you know that you've got to make time for your investments. But how?

Let's look at your schedule: Okay, drive Tony to his baseball practice, pick up the dry cleaning, stop at the grocery store, and . . . what's this? You're not doing anything from 3:59 P.M. to 4:07 P.M. Imagine that: a full eight minutes to yourself! With that kind of free time on your hands, you can sit down at the kitchen table and balance the U.S. budget!

Okay, so you're busy. But before you toss out the idea of working on your investments along with last week's wilted lettuce, consider this: You can get tips on what kind of stocks to buy while you're going about your daily routine.

Forget the Lotto. You've Got Millions in the House.

As you prepare dinner for the family, you open the pantry and grab four cans of Campbell's minestrone soup. Campbell's soup? Mmm. Mmm. Good idea! When it comes to soup, Campbell's is the undisputed brand-name king. For the main dish, you head to the fridge for the Hillshire Farms ham. Setting it on a baking dish bought at Wal-Mart, you stick the ham in the oven to be warmed up. Dessert? A Sara Lee French silk pie will do nicely. You set it out on the kitchen countertop, made of materials bought from Home Depot. There you go: Not only do you have a nice dinner in the wings, you've also got four stock tips.

If you invested $1,000 in Campbell's Soup in 1985, it would amount to about $15,000 today. A grand in Sara Lee, which owns Hillshire Farms, would become $16,000. How about Wal-Mart? Hold on to your hats: If you had put $1,000 in the retailer in 1983, you'd have more than $3 million today. The same amount in Home Depot in 1981 would give you more than $1 million now.

Two-thirds of all outstanding stocks are companies that sell goods and services used by consumers. Wouldn't it be nice if we could turn back the clock and put money in these companies when they were still small? If you could go back, you probably wouldn't even be cooking today—you'd have a private chef! But since we can't blast to the past, let's do the next best thing: invest now in the up-and-coming companies of the future.

How do we invest in a company? One way is to buy its stock.

A Special Brownie and One Smart Cookie

Let's go to the island of Nantucket and visit with a widow named Mrs. Wiggybottom. As the best baker in her neighborhood, her specialty was a milk-chocolate brownie with a butter-caramel center and dusted with powdered sugar. It came from a centuries-old recipe handed down from her great-grandmother. For years only family and friends knew about her melt-in-your-mouth brownie. One day a salesman came to her house, hoping to sell shower curtains. She didn't buy any, but being the hospitable lady she was, Mrs. Wiggybottom couldn't let the nice gentleman leave without some refreshments. She offered him a cup of tea and one of her special brownies. After one delicious bite, the salesman immediately tasted the marketing potential.

He convinced Mrs. Wiggybottom that she should sell the brownie across America, with him as her agent. They started by marketing to neighborhood grocers who agreed to carry a few samples after a bit of smooth talking by the agent and a taste of the brownie. In a year Mrs. Wiggybottom's Brownies sold out in supermarkets all over the island. Success put her in a tizzy. Why, she was baking as furiously as she could and still barely met orders! Her home became a mini-warehouse overflowing with boxes of brownies, stacked floor to ceiling in the living room, den, garage— you name it.

It was time to organize her business. Calling her fledgling company Heavenly Delights Inc., Mrs. Wiggybottom borrowed money from family and friends to open a small office, lease a commercial kitchen, and hire workers. Sales continued to skyrocket—her brownies were now reaching supermarkets all over Massachusetts. With orders piling up, she soon needed even more funds to expand—the kind beyond the pockets of people close to her. She approached the local banker, who gave her a loan.

Five years later, to her delight, Mrs. Wiggybottom's Brownies became a household name like Sara Lee. The small office had given way to a spiffy glass-and-chrome building and Mrs. Wiggybottom conducted business at an impressive corner office with a view. The good lady from Nantucket, who for years never even thought beyond her neighborhood, now set about to conquer the country. At least, the part that likes dessert. She expanded into a line of cake mixes, frostings, pies, frozen cookie dough, and ice cream. The next frontier was retail: Mrs. W's Bakery and Tea Room.

But expanding took money. This time Mrs. Wiggybottom decided to get funds, or capital, from a different source. Since she already borrowed from family, friends, and the bank, she turned to two new options: bonds and stocks.

Bonds Are Not Secret Agents

Bond? James Bond? 007? I'm afraid not. A bond isn't an agent on Her Majesty's Secret Service who totes guns and women with equal ease. Quite simply, it's an IOU. When a company sells bonds to investors, it gives them certificates in exchange for a loan. The certificates promise that the loan will be repaid at the end of the bond's life or term. Meanwhile, investors get interest payments twice a year for their trouble. You've heard of government savings bonds? It's really an IOU from Uncle Sam. Today, since everything is electronic, investors typically don't get an actual certificate (although they could). Instead, they get a report or account statement that proves bond ownership.

If you had bought the corporate bonds of a small business like Heavenly Delights, you could get anywhere from 5 to 14 percent interest or even higher, depending on the stability of the company. The bond's life span—also called maturity—could range from several weeks to one hundred years, but the typical time frame is one to twenty years. An investor in corporate bonds will receive interest payments and get back her principal when the bonds mature, providing the company survives.

That's the usual scenario. There are many other facets to bonds that we won't explore here (for instance, not all of them pay interest) because we want to focus on stocks as the most lucrative and viable investment for most people.

So Heavenly Delights issued bonds to raise money, and it sufficed for a few years. But soon Mrs. Wiggybottom became concerned that the company was borrowing too much. After all, debt has to be repaid. She decided it was time to sell stock.

What's Stock Got to Do With It?

When a company offers its stock to the public for the first time, it's called an *initial public offering* or *IPO*.

A single stock—also called a share—represents part ownership of a company. If Mrs. Wiggybottom decides to sell Heavenly Delights stock to the public, it's like chopping up her firm into little pieces and selling each piece to the highest bidder. The result:

The company will raise money for business and investors will receive stock, which makes them part owners or shareholders of the company. Like bonds, shares can come as a certificate. But most people choose to get an account statement showing ownership instead. It's simpler.

To go public, Heavenly Delights found a professional underwriter to handle the process. Together, they looked at Heavenly Delights and compared it with similar companies in the industry to arrive at an approximate price range for the stock. Heavenly Delights also figured out how much money it needed and the investment banker recommended selling a certain number of shares. The investment banker, as the underwriter, looks around for potential buyers and gauges their interest. After all this research, it was agreed that Heavenly Delights should go public at $5 a share and sell 10 million shares.

Let's say Myrtle, a friend from Mrs. Wiggybottom's bridge club, decided to buy a thousand shares of the company. A smart investor, she believed her purchase of Heavenly Delights at $5 a share—or $5,000 total for one thousand shares—was a good investment because she could make a profit if the price went higher.

Although Myrtle knew there were no guarantees, she was confident the stock price would rise because Heavenly Delights was a good company with solid earnings. She had done her homework. Surely such a company would be attractive to other investors and they too would want to buy the stock. When many people want to purchase the same thing, its price rises. Who could forget the fuss over Cabbage Patch dolls? Parents outbid and even fought each other to get one.

If the stock price of Heavenly Delights rises higher than $5, *Myrtle can sell her stock at a gain.* Who can she sell to? The company usually doesn't buy it back, although it might sometimes. In most cases, an investor like Myrtle has to sell it to another investor. It's just like selling your home. You don't hand it back to the real-estate developer, do you? You sell it to someone else who wants to own it.

A Stock Table Is Not Furniture

One day Heavenly Delights hit $15.50 a share. That was the highest it had ever reached in a year. The company was riding high—its products were sold out all over the country. People loved the Mrs. Wiggybottom brand and retailers were lining up to stock these desserts. The media started taking notice too. Mrs. Wiggybottom landed on the cover of a business magazine with the headline MRS. W AND HER GROWING EMPIRE. The story came out at the same time as Heavenly Delights' earnings report. Profits doubled from the previous year. So it came as no surprise when the stock hit $15.50 a share—its highest in fifty-two weeks or the fifty-two-week high. When a momentous event such as this occurs, the media report it. Conversely, a stock that hits its lowest point in the last twelve months is said to be at the fifty-two-week low.

Myrtle heard the news and grabbed the local paper to check. She flipped to the stock tables in the business section—pages and pages of numbers flowing from top to bottom—and looked up Heavenly Delights. Myrtle checked the "Closing Price" column to get the stock's ending price yesterday. There it was: 15½. Since prices are quoted in fractions, 15½ means $15.50 a share.

| Stock & Symbol | Closing Price | Chg. | Day's Price | |
			High	Low
Heavenly Delights HVLY	15½	+2	15½	13

Myrtle also checked the change or "Chg." column. The "+2" means the stock went up by two dollars to close at 15½. Heavenly Delights rose by two bucks yesterday after it announced healthy profits for the year. It was time to cash out some of the stock.

Myrtle decided to sell one hundred shares. The next day she was able to get 15¼ or $15.25 per share. Her profit would be $10.25 a share ($15.25 minus her purchase price of $5 a share) for a windfall of $1,025 before taxes and broker fees! If she sold all one thousand shares, her profit would be $10,250—more than double the $5,000 she invested three years ago! No bank CDs pay this kind of interest. If they did, the banks would go out of business.

Good Company + Good Timing = Great Investment

Myrtle's key to success is that she picked a good stock to buy *and* she bought it at the right time. You want to do the same thing: choose a stock whose price has a good potential of rising and then read its price charts for the best time to jump in. What makes a stock price rise? It advances if investors believe the company's business will get stronger in the future. Maybe there's a hot product, new management, or strong company profits.

Let's go back to our example of owning a home. What makes a house more valuable? Remodeling, add-ons, or its location in a growing neighborhood. Imagine that you bought a three-bedroom, 2.5-bath home for $100,000 in the beach community of Santa Monica, California, twenty years ago. Then little Bobby arrived, followed by curly-haired Sue. They needed separate rooms, so you built an extra bedroom and bath. While you were at it, maybe the patio needed a little work. How about adding a pool too? Meanwhile, you noticed more people were moving into your neighborhood, attracted by its proximity to the beach. Today, your house is worth roughly $500,000—higher than your neighbors'—thanks to upgrades, additions, and market trends.

Owning a stock is like being a homeowner. You want to own shares of a company that is "remodeling," "adding on," or "in a growing neighborhood." That means you want companies whose businesses are improving and in a growing industry. We'll go over the key success factors of a stock in Chapter 4.

A good example is Wal-Mart. The retailer caught your eye because every time you visited a store, it was always crowded. Shoppers *loved* Wal-Mart's deals—whether it was laundry detergent for $3.99, bras priced at $6.99, or a satin blouse selling for $17.99. After a little homework, you discovered that the retailer has added a new product—in recent years it began to raid the supermarkets' turf by selling groceries. You also looked at other ways Wal-Mart was excelling and thought of buying the stock. Wouldn't it be great if you spotted Wal-Mart when it was still a small store chain in Arkansas? You could have bought the stock cheap—and reaped a fortune today!

Shopping for Sizes: Small, Medium, or Large?

Just as you can buy a small, medium, or large home, stocks come in different sizes as well. Big companies are called large-capitalization or simply large-cap stocks. These are companies worth $10 billion or more in the market. If someone were to buy them, that's how much they would cost. You probably know many large-caps by name: Ford, McDonald's, and IBM, for example. How do Wall Street professionals know they're each worth $10 billion or more? It's easy: Multiply the number of shares a company has by its stock price. If it has 200 million shares and the stock trades at $50—bingo, that's $10 billion. "But I don't have $10 billion!" you say. No, but you can buy a piece of the company.

If you'd like to stay in a mansion in the suburbs of Charlotte but can't afford the entire $2.5 million home, what do you do? You might look into buying a timeshare. For $8,000, you can pretend to be Scarlett O'Hara and live in luxury for one week every year. In the same way, you may not be able to buy the entire Coca-Cola Co., but you can own some of its shares.

If you prefer medium or small companies, there are names for them too. Medium-sized firms are called mid-capitalization stocks or simply mid-caps. These are businesses worth between $1.5 billion and $10 billion. Finally, small-caps are valued at $1.5 billion or less. Historically, investors in these companies enjoy the best average returns on their money because successful smaller businesses tend to grow faster than large corporations.

It makes sense: Heavenly Delights can grow faster than Sara Lee because Mrs. Wiggybottom's company is just starting to take off. It hasn't saturated the market yet. It would be easier for Heavenly Delights to show a 100 percent increase in sales—from $3 million to $6 million—than it would be for Sara Lee to go from $5 billion to $10 billion.

The Stock Market: It's Just a Giant Swap Meet

Stocks are bought and sold at a stock exchange. Think of it as a giant swap meet. The exchange is an actual location where hordes of people meet to do business. At the exchange, buyers and sellers of stocks haggle over prices—usually while making wild gestures and yelling at each other. You've probably seen a stock exchange on the evening news.

You, as an investor, won't go to the exchange itself. You'll be represented by floor brokers who get commissions for their services—they don't get pushed around and hollered at for free!

The most prestigious exchange is located in New York, aptly called the New York Stock Exchange. Stocks of the biggest and most established companies are listed here—this is their main marketplace. Also nicknamed "The Big Board," NYSE began when people met under a cottonwood tree to do business by a wall that used to keep animals in, hence the name "Wall Street." Today, Wall Street is the main thoroughfare in New York City's financial district. It is famous worldwide for its capital markets.

Aside from NYSE, there's also the American Stock Exchange and various regional exchanges throughout the country. Like the Big Board, these exchanges are actual locations.

Then there's NASDAQ, also called the over-the-counter market. Like an exchange, it's a marketplace where people buy and sell. However, instead of a physical location such as New York, all the trading is done by computer. Imagine a web of computers linked with each other across the country. Using this system, brokerage firms can buy and sell stocks. While the NYSE is the most famous exchange, many prestigious firms such as Microsoft and Intel choose to list on the NASDAQ.

To make trading simpler, companies are identified by a "nickname." General Electric is "GE," AT&T is "T," and United Airlines is "UAL." These names are called "ticker symbols" because they used to run on a ticker tape—a running piece of paper that lists stocks and their prices. Today, we use an electronic ticker that runs on the walls of the exchanges.

If a company is listed on the New York, American, or regional exchanges, it is identified by three or fewer letters. NASDAQ gives its stocks four or more letters.

Finding a Broker

To buy and sell stocks, you need a broker. You can't do it yourself; the government allows only registered companies and individuals to make the actual trades.

So who is a broker? A broker is a licensed individual who buys and sells securities (things like stocks and bonds) for you. They work for brokerage firms such as Charles Schwab, E*Trade, Merrill Lynch, and Salomon Smith Barney. Think of them as your personal shopper. All you need to do is tell them what you want and they'll do your bidding. Of course, you have to pay them a commission.

To get a broker, you need to open an account with a brokerage firm by phoning them, visiting their office, by mail, or e-mailing the company. They'll give you an application form to fill out—and they will ask for information on your finances. You also may have to deposit money in the account before you trade.

There are two types of accounts: cash and margin. A cash account means you'll pay for your trades by check or use the money you deposited in the account at your brokerage. A margin account is when you'll put up some money and borrow the rest from the brokerage firm for your trades. Of course, you'll have to pay interest on the loan. People like to trade on margin because it could magnify their gains. After all, they're trading with more money than they have in the first place. But it's much riskier, since the losses are magnified as well.

Once you're a customer, you can place trades with your broker—ask him or her to buy and sell for you.

You can choose among many types of brokerage firms. There are the full-service brokers—upscale companies that charge more because they give you advice as well as execute your trades. These are the Saks Fifth Avenues of brokerage houses. Then there are the JC Penneys of the industry: the discount brokers. They charge less, but they don't give you advice. They'll buy and sell for you, and that's pretty much it. Finally, there are the online brokers. You trade with them through the Internet and they cost the least—like a Dollar Store.

As the most economical, online brokers have found a large fan club among small investors. They include E*Trade, Ameritrade, and Datek. Their popularity has prompted many full-service and discount brokers to offer online services as well. DLJ is a full-service house that also offers DLJ Direct, its online brokerage operation. Waterhouse Securities is a discount house; its online arm is called WebBroker.

To find a broker that best fits your needs, first determine your expectations. If you want advice, plenty of research done for you, and access to a wider variety of financial products, choose a full-service broker but be prepared to pay substantially higher fees. On the other hand, if you're comfortable investing by yourself, a discount or online broker will suffice. A discount broker will offer fewer services and products than full-service brokers, but their rates are cheaper since they make money by volume. You may call a discount broker to place trades, but don't expect any advice. Online brokers offer the best deal of all. To get the lowest fees you have to place your trades through the Internet. Online brokers also let you place your orders by phone or fax, usually for a higher fee.

Picking a full-service broker may seem to make the best sense. After all, you might argue, it's okay to pay more as long as you'll get the best return for your money. The problem is this: Full-service brokers don't always invest better because they act more like salespeople than investment experts. Their recommendations are hit-and-miss.

The Running of the Bulls

Ding, ding, ding! It's 9:30 A.M. in the Big Apple and the Big Board has just opened for business. Immediately, a swarm of uniformed people—mostly men—jostle, yell, and crowd against each other on the floor. The electronic ticker overhead comes alive: Glowing letters and numbers careen across the black screen as they show the opening prices of the day. Big money is being made and lost every trading day.

Believe it or not, it all really begins with you, the investor. *Moi?* Little old me with my $1,000 in savings? Yes, you. I'll show you how. Let's go visit with Ruby Rutherford of Omaha. As she checks a stock she's had her eye on for a while, she spots a pattern on its price chart that tells her it's time to invest. She's ready, having studied and researched diligently. The only thing left to do is take the plunge. She picks up the phone and calls her broker.

For weeks, Ruby has favored Netbank. Not only is it a promising Internet bank that offers higher passbook rates, but the industry's future looks golden. Her phone call goes through. "Hi. This is Ruby Rutherford," she says. "How much is NTBK selling for right now? Good. I'd like to buy ten shares, at $50 a share." NTBK is the ticker symbol or "nickname" for Netbank.

Ruby has just placed a "limit" order, which specifies a price to buy or sell. The broker has to meet this price or do better for the trade to go through. Ruby didn't want to put in a "market" order, because the broker will try to buy the shares at whatever price it's being traded at the moment and it could be way off her budget. Other types of orders are: "sell at a limit," where your broker will sell the shares only at the price you set or better; "sell at market," where shares are sold at the prevailing market price; and "sell at a stop limit," which tells your broker to sell when the stock falls to a certain price. For example, if you buy Pfizer at $42 and set a sell stop of $38, it means your broker will sell the stock if it falls to $38.

Thousands of miles away, Pablo Estevez in Miami decides to sell ten shares of his Netbank stock because he needs some money to landscape his backyard. He calls up his broker, gets a stock quote or price, and puts in a sell-at-market order. As he pulls weeds in his garden, he waits for the order to be filled.

From their offices, Ruby's and Pablo's brokers send their orders to the stock exchange floor. The trades, one to buy and one to sell, are routed to the floor brokers. Remember them? They're the ones who shove and shout at each other. The floor broker representing Ruby and the one for Pablo compete with other brokers to find the best prices for their clients. Finally, Ruby's and Pablo's floor brokers meet and agree on a price.

While all this is happening, the orders are scrutinized by a *specialist*. A specialist is a person who makes sure trading goes on in an orderly manner. Not only that, he or she is critical in bridging gaps. If a broker's order to buy can't be matched with a sell order, or the other way around, the specialist may step in and accept it. A specialist ensures that investors like Ruby and Pablo won't be left in the lurch.

This time the specialist's help isn't needed. The deal is done—

Ruby has bought Pablo's ten shares of Netbank for $49 each. The limit price was set at $50 a share but the floor broker was able to do better at $49, so the deal was done. Within three days, Ruby must make sure her payment and commission for NTBK is in the broker's hands. As for Pablo? The broker deposits the money into his account, after taking out the commission.

That's how a trade is made at an exchange. In NASDAQ transactions, the specialist is replaced by *market makers*. These are brokerage firms that have an inventory of different stocks. If Ruby and Pablo went through NASDAQ, instead of selling to each other, Ruby would have to sell to a market maker and Pablo would have to buy from a market maker. The market maker is the middleman in the deal. It makes a profit from each trade.

It's Worth Repeating

Let's recap for a moment, shall we? A stock represents part ownership of a company. It is bought and sold—or traded—at a marketplace called a stock exchange, or through NASDAQ. The stock price rises if investors believe that a company's prospects look good. To get a stock's price, look up the company in the stock tables of a financial newspaper such as *The Wall Street Journal*. Investors who want to know the price at any moment during the trading day may call their brokers, watch a financial news show, or search the Internet. A broker buys and sells stock and other investments for a commission.

Now you understand how the market works. Broken down into basics, it's just a collection of buy and sell orders from all over the world. There's no special mystery to it. Yet, for the longest time, this was a marketplace tapped only by wealthy men. People with meager savings, as well as most women, did not belong to this club. The stock market was the rich guy's "secret."

But now we know what they know. The Internet revolution has made it even easier to access financial data today and it has fueled a growth in individual investing. If a little knowledge is a dangerous thing, what about a lot of knowledge? For wild Wall Street women, it means this: Watch out investment world, we are stampeding through!

CHAPTER THREE

Scavenger Hunt: Narrowing Down Your Choices

Ready? Small, excited faces turn up expectantly. *Get set.* Little feet shuffle in nervous excitement on the grass. *Go!* With a squeal, the children fan out over the garden looking for clues in the scavenger hunt. Remember those days? You'd huff and puff all over the place to be the first to find the prize—a new Barbie, a shiny yo-yo, or a bucket of Legos. Whatever it was, the trek was worth the effort. You loved it.

Let's go on an adult scavenger hunt. This time the prize is a secure financial future. If you plan it right, you could retire with millions. But first, we have to look for clues to winning stocks that you can bank on. They're everywhere—on the Internet, in the stock tables of a financial newspaper, in stock reports at the public library, tips you hear from friends, or businesses you enjoy patronizing.

While you're searching for candidates, keep this picture in mind:

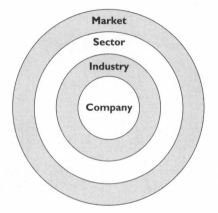

We want to look at every aspect of the bull's-eye when we hunt for our winning stock. Start with the outermost ring, called the *market*. The market is the stockmarket universe. It is the giant swap meet where all the stocks are bought and sold. In this swap meet, there are many buyers and sellers. When there are more buyers than sellers, the trades to purchase stocks will outnumber the trades to sell stocks. Therefore, the market will rise. If sellers outnumber buyers, the market will fall. *We want a market that is going up.* For us to buy stocks, we want the market to be good. It will increase the likelihood of our stock's success because there are many people buying shares. If it's a down market, wait it out. Don't buy.

You can tell whether we're in an up market by looking at charts for the Dow Jones Industrial Average, the Standard & Poor's 500, and the NASDAQ Composite Index. These indices measure the movement of the market. We'll discuss them in detail in Chapter 6. For now, look for their charts in the front page of *The Wall Street Journal*'s Money & Investing section. We want the three charts to show rising trends. If the three don't agree on direction—

one may be pointing down but two are going up—follow the S&P 500. Historically, it leads the other two.

On the Internet, you may check on the market by clicking on the indices at www.yahoo.com, www.bigchart.com, www.zacks.com, www.bloomberg.com, and www.askresearch.com. The ticker symbol for the Dow is $INDU, SPX for the S&P 500, and COMP for the NASDAQ Composite.

If you're not on the Internet, I highly recommend that you get on. It is the best place to get free investment research—an avalanche of financial information is at your fingertips. You can also monitor your stocks easily, without having to wait until the next day's paper. As an incentive, personal computer prices have been dropping dramatically. Subscribing to Internet access is free through www.netzero.net. A paid Internet service provider costs about $20 a month. If you don't think you'll be using the computer enough to justify getting one, many public libraries should provide free access.

My favorite financial Web sites are www.marketguide.com, www.marketwatch.com, www.yahoo.com, www.rapidresearch.com, www.wallstreetcity.com, www.bigcharts.com, and www.financial web.com. Take some time to familiarize yourself with them. If you want to tap other sites, do a search. New ones may come online after this book is published.

The second ring in the bull's-eye is *sector*. A sector is a segment of the U.S. economy. Examples of sectors are technology, energy, consumer cyclical, financial, and health care. We want to choose a sector that's hot—doing well and in demand by investors. If the sector attracts investors, money should pour into companies within the sector. As more people buy stocks in the sector, prices should increase more here than in the others.

You could go to www.marketguide.com and scroll down to

"What's Hot." Click on that, then click on sectors. To choose a hot sector, look under the "EPS Qtr. vs. Yr. Ago" column, which shows the percentage growth of profits in a sector. Next, scan the "Rev. Qtr. vs. Yr. Ago" column, which shows the percentage growth of sales. Finally, check under "5 Day Price Chg."—it tells you how much the price has appreciated. Jot down two sectors that show the highest numbers in the three columns.

In the chart on page 37, technology looks like the strongest sector with a five-day price change of 3.9 percent, profit growth (EPS) of 34.8 percent, and revenue or sales growth of 27.7 percent. The second strongest is health care. Its five-day price change is 0.4 percent, profits rose 16.7 percent, and revenue went up by 21.1 percent. Rounding out the top three is the services sector, with a five-day price increase of 0.2 percent, profit gains of 17.6 percent, and revenue increases of 19 percent. Once you pick a few sectors, click on them to find the top industries within.

Industry is our third ring. An industry is a smaller subset of a sector. For example, the banking industry would fall under the larger purview of the financial sector. So would the brokerage and insurance industries. Apply the rules we used for sectors— the higher the profits, sales, and price performance, the better the industry looks. Choose the top industry in each of the three sectors.

If you're not online, find the nearest public library that sub-scribes to Value Line investment reports. Value Line comes in two editions, but let's start with the *Value Line Investment Survey*. In the first few pages, you'll run across a ranking of industries in terms of timeliness. That means they're rated according to how well the industries are expected to perform. The higher an industry is ranked, the better are its expectations of showing the best price

WHAT'S HOT/WHAT'S NOT

All data as of July 14, 1999

Sector Price Performance

Sector	1 Day Price Chg %	5 Day Price Chg %	P/E	Div. Yield (%)	Price to Book	ROE (%)	Debt to Equity	Rev. Qtr vs Yr Ago	EPS Qtr vs Yr Ago
Technology	1.8	3.9	54.1	0.6	15.6	24.2	0.4	27.7	34.8
Capital Goods	0.5	0.8	20.8	1.5	3.7	16.8	1.1	12.1	10.6
Consumer/Noncyclical	0.4	1.0	33.9	1.9	10.8	32.6	1.4	5.3	6.3
Energy	0.3	0.7	46.3	2.2	3.8	5.1	0.7	−10.0	−38.6
Consumer/Cyclical	0.3	−1.5	19.6	2.1	4.2	20.0	2.1	12.2	0.1
Transportation	0.3	−1.1	17.7	1.3	2.9	15.8	1.0	8.7	8.6
Conglomerates	0.3	−1.1	35.7	1.3	8.2	24.1	3.2	8.4	16.6
Services	0.3	0.2	34.1	1.6	6.8	15.1	1.2	19.0	17.6
Utilities	0.1	0.0	18.9	4.2	2.3	10.3	1.5	9.4	13.1
Health Care	0.0	0.4	43.6	1.2	12.9	28.4	0.5	21.1	16.7
Basic Materials	0.0	0.5	30.9	1.9	4.2	11.2	1.2	5.6	3.9
Financial	−0.4	−2.0	22.6	1.7	4.0	16.8	NM	13.1	18.5

Source: www.marketguide.com

increases in the next six to twelve months. Therefore, we want to pick industries among the top three.

You may also take a peek at *Value Line Selection & Opinion*. On the Market Monitor page, there's a list of the best performing industries in terms of stock price increases.

The idea is to find a hot industry. You're going to come across several good ones—that's okay. Right now we're just shopping around. Keep your eye on a few industries.

Finally, we get to the bull's-eye: *companies*. After choosing our top sectors and industries, we want to find the best companies in those areas. After all, we want the honor roll, not stocks at the bottom of the class. Click on the top industries and look at the companies listed. Again, profits, sales, and price performance determine your candidates. Pick as many as you would feel comfortable following, perhaps three.

If you're not online, go back to the *Value Line Investment Survey*. Go past the industry rankings and look for listings of companies under each industry. We want stocks that are ranked one or two for timeliness, meaning they are expected to be among the best performers in the next year.

To get a second opinion on the companies you choose, ask the library for the Standard & Poor's stock reports. Find your stock in the alphabetical listing and flip to its profile. On the top left-hand side, it will say "S&P Opinion." We want stocks with a five- or four-star rating. Five means buy, four means accumulate.

Keep in mind that you don't have to start with the outer ring, the market, all the time. It doesn't matter where you start, *as long as you look at all the rings*. So if Uncle Louie tells you that Billy's Bagels is a good buy, you know what to do: Look up the company, industry, sector, and market.

The stock tables in a financial publication or the local paper provide good stock tips too. Look for companies hitting fifty-two-week highs. Investors are buying those companies for a reason, and you should find out why. Some business publications also list stocks with the highest gains in volume—the number of shares traded. If a stock has high volume and the price is rising, that means many investors are buying it. Something's cooking. We'll talk more about volume in Chapter 5.

The www.rapidresearch.com site lists the top-twenty growth stocks. Pick companies with the best profits.

To get ideas from www.marketwatch.com, click on its fifty-two week Highs and Lows section and pick out stocks hitting new highs. Also look for ideas in Dollar Volume Leaders and Broker Research. In the Insider Trading section, look for key executives buying their company's stock. If company insiders want to accumulate more stock, they're optimistic about business.

Feel free to search other financial Web sites for ideas, *as long as you get the best companies in the best industries within the best sectors in a rising market.* A tall order? Not really. If you can spend an entire day organizing your closet, you can certainly spare an hour to map out your financial future.

Some people like the message boards at the Yahoo Web site. There, you can get a feel for a company by listening to what other investors have to say. Another popular site is www.silicon-investor.com, which is known for tech stock talk. Also, don't forget to check the message boards at www.fool.com.

As you scan more stocks, you'll get a sense of which one is a good candidate. But we're not ready to buy yet; the stock has to go through more rigorous scrutiny, as we shall see in the next chapter. However, a cursory examination is enough in the candidate-gathering stage.

Now let's practice. Go to Market Guide Inc.'s Web site at

www.marketguide.com and click on "What's Hot" first and "Sectors" next. We'll see a long list of hot sectors. Let's pick technology because it had strong profits. Clicking on technology, we see many industries. We'll choose the computer hardware industry because it's also a big profit maker. Clicking on computer hardware, we get a long line of companies. After quickly scanning the "EPS Qtr.," "Rev Qtr.," and the "5 Day" columns, we winnow our choices down to five stocks.

Value Line and Standard & Poor's may have profiles of the companies. Online, go to www.marketwatch.com, punch in the ticker symbols to get a quick snapshot of the company. We want to get acquainted with these companies.

Inevitably, while researching a company, you'll stumble across business news about them. Pay attention to announcements of new products, new management, or pending mergers and acquisitions. A promising new product could boost sales; new managers might infuse much-needed vitality into a company, especially if they've got successful track records. As for mergers and acquisitions, it's typical for the stock of the company *being absorbed* to rise after such an announcement. Investors rush to buy the stock of the sold company, expecting the buyer to pay a premium for it.

Watch for companies announcing share buybacks. That means they'll buy their stock back from investors. It's good news because it means a company has the money to buy the stock. The stock price will most likely appreciate because there will be fewer shares out there for investors to fight over. Theoretically, with less supply and the same or greater demand, the stock should rise. To check on buybacks, go to www.marketwatch.com.

Finally, keep reading about the companies. The more you know, the better off you'll be. Don't feel pressured to pick among the candidates right now. We'll look at them in more detail with the system I'll teach you in the next chapter.

CHAPTER FOUR

Finding the Right Stock

Stella stared at herself in the mirror at the beauty salon and saw dark roots peeking from beneath her auburn locks. She should have had a touch-up a month ago, but things were just so hectic at work. Good thing her hairdresser, Tina, was adept at making the color last as long as it did. As the stylist wrapped foil around strands of her hair, Stella picked up a magazine to read. But suddenly she felt a hand on her shoulder.

"Guess what?" Tina said with excitement. "I've started investing and I'm making money! I even watch business news now. Can you believe it? Me?" Stella listened with interest. It's what she has been itching to do too—get into the stock market. But she just never knew where to start and what to buy. Tina made it sound so easy. Better yet, she passed along a tip from a friend that Pete's Bicycle Co. was a good stock to buy. Her friend knew someone at the company who said business was great and the stock was bound to appreciate.

Two hours later Stella left the salon with a new hairdo and a new conviction: She was going to do it—jump into the market.

With $2,000 of her hard-earned savings, Stella bought one hundred shares of Pete's Bicycle at 19¾ (or $19.75) a share and paid $25 in broker fees. She faithfully followed her stock every day, hoping for a windfall. But it didn't come. After two months Pete's dropped to $16. She thought about selling, but didn't want to take the loss. Another six months passed and Pete's had tumbled to $10. Finally, Stella sold it. She lost $1,025, including commissions.

What happened? Stella's mistake was buying a stock without a proper investment strategy. That's gambling, not investing. It's fine to get stock tips from friends, but it's often fatal to make a purchase without any research.

If Stella had properly evaluated stocks using tools that have proven to be effective historically, she would have increased her chances of success.

These tools can be remembered in a simple acronym: "BE A PROFIT." It stands for *B*eta, *E*arnings, *A*tmosphere, *P*rice performance, *R*eturn on Equity, *O*utstanding performer, *F*loat, *I*nstitutional ownership, and *T*op dollar. These are aspects of a company an investor should consider before buying its stock. Although there are more factors one may consider in a stock, "BE A PROFIT" forms the core. You can find each of these characteristics in Value Line reports, stock tables of a financial newspaper, and at various financial Web sites.

A Checklist for Winning Stocks

Women are great with lists. There's something so neat, tidy, and comforting about a checklist. It's small enough to slip into a purse yet it carries enormous consequences for our lives. Don't you feel tension slip slowly away as you check off each item on your to-do list during a busy-as-usual day? The list assures you that you're on track and you didn't forget anything.

I'm going to show you how to use a checklist to help you determine whether a particular stock is a good investment.

Write the letters B-E-A-P-R-O-F-I-T down, like this:

Co. name	B	E	A	P	R	O	F	I	T

Each letter stands for a standard that a company has to meet. As the stock fulfills each requirement, put a check mark underneath it. If it doesn't, put an X instead. The more check marks you see on your page, the higher your odds of having a good investment candidate. Let's go over each letter.

B Is for Beta

Beta? "That's Greek to me," you mumble. You're right! It is Greek. Beta is the second letter in the Greek alphabet. In investing, beta has a special meaning. It is a statistical measure of 1) a stock's past price swings, and compares it with 2) the change in the market, usually as measured by the Standard & Poor's 500 index. "Yuck," you say. "That *is* Greek to me!"

Let's make it simple. Beta measures a stock's risk. How? By comparing a stock's price movements to swings in the market. A stock that swings more wildly than the market will have a higher beta than one that doesn't. Therefore, the wilder stock is riskier than the tame stock. (Such price swings are called *volatility*.) Usually, beta is calculated over three years.

When you see a stock with a high beta, you know that it's a wild thing. That's its nature. When the market goes up, it will rise higher. But if the market drops, it will dip lower. It's like an emotionally sensitive child who either blows up in anger or laughs uproariously in joy: The stock overreacts compared with the market. Conversely, a low-beta stock won't react as much: When the market rises, it won't increase as much; when the market declines, it also won't drop as much. This is like a timid child. She keeps her emotions hidden. She doesn't react to events as much as you would expect.

Why bother with beta? When you're choosing between two stocks of the same caliber but one has a higher beta than the other, picking the lower beta will expose you to less risk. However, you're also giving up the potential of greater riches. Let me explain.

First, understand that beta comes in numbers. The stock market's movement is given a beta of 1. When a stock also has a beta of 1, it swings as much as the market. When the market moves up a little, so will the stock. If the market goes down by a lot, thus follows the stock.

A stock with a beta above or below 1 tells investors how far a stock has deviated from the market as a whole. For example, if a stock's beta is 1.5, it will go up or down as much as one and a half times more than the market. If the beta is 0.5, the stock is expected to go up or down half as much. Technology stocks typically have betas much greater than 1. Utilities fall under 1 because their prices have historically been more stable.

Let's say you thought about buying a computer stock with a beta of 2. You know it could go up or down twice as much as the market. If the market, as measured by the movement of the Standard & Poor's 500, is up 5 percent, then the stock could move up twice as much, or by 10 percent. If the S&P is down by 5 percent, then your stock could drop by as much as 10 percent.

More aggressive investors would like this stock. They don't mind taking the risks because the reward is sweeter.

Maybe your stomach can't take it. If so, you might prefer a retail company, which tends to be less volatile than computer stocks. If its beta is 1.3, that means the stock is going to move up or down 30 percent more than the market. Therefore, if the market is down by 5 percent, your stock is expected to go down as much as 6.5 percent (5 percent × 1.3). But if the market rises by 5 percent, your stock gains by 6.5 percent.

A stock with a beta below 1—that is, below the market—means that it swings *less* wildly than the market. This is a low-beta stock. If a food company you like has a beta of 0.8, that means its stock price is going to move up or down 20 percent less than the market (0.8 is 20 percent less than 1). Therefore, if the market drops by 5 percent, your stock should dip by no more than 4 percent (5 percent × 0.8). But if the market rises by 5 percent, your stock only gains 4 percent.

To sum it up: The higher the beta, the higher the risk and the promise of rewards. The lower the beta, the lower the risk and there's less reward as well.

If you imagine the stock market's beta as a straight line, this is how the computer stock with a beta of 2 would have swung:

COMPUTER STOCK
(Beta = 2)

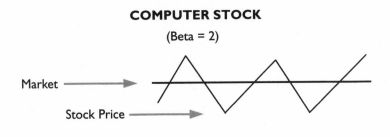

Market

Stock Price

Here's how the retail stock would have fared:

RETAIL STOCK
(Beta = 1.3)

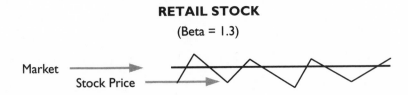

Market

Stock Price

Aggressive investors don't mind the wild ride on the computer stock. They can take the lows as long as there's a chance to hit a high. However, conservative investors would prefer lower-beta stocks like the retail company. They don't mind giving up greater riches as long as there's less risk.

I'm not saying that higher-beta stocks are only for gamblers and you should aim for a beta of less than 1. Higher-beta stocks will get you higher returns. But if you're faced with two good candidates, the lower-beta stock will let you sleep better at night. If you decide to own a high-beta stock, keep a close eye on it and get ready to sell quickly—since the tide could turn sharply and suddenly.

Don't be too quick to buy a stock with a beta of 2 and higher. Studies have found that less than 5 percent of the best stocks carried this level of volatility. Therefore, don't take any more risks than you can comfortably tolerate. Studies have shown that the best stocks have had an average beta of 1.14. (Beta ratings are found in a stock report.)

When you've researched the beta of a stock, check "B" and write down its beta grade next to it.

E Is for Earnings

It's another word for profit, net income, or the bottom line. Four words or phrases that mean the same thing? Yes. *Earnings are the money left over after a company pays its expenses.*

Let's say that Brooke's Bikinis for Big Beautiful Women sold $5 million worth of swimsuits last year. But the company doesn't get to pocket all $5 million in sales (also called revenue). After all, it has many expenses. There are the salaries of the one hundred employees. There's Bob Marshall, the wholesaler from whom Brooke buys the material for her bathing suits. There's the landlord, the utility company, and so on. Uncle Sam has his hand out too, since Brooke has to pay taxes. After she takes out business costs, the company is left with $100,000. That's earnings—what the company *really* made.

"Why do you look at earnings when sales are more impressive?" you ask. Sure, sales look good. But if Brooke ends up with no earnings, what good is having a lot of sales? Her business won't last. Imagine that instead of making $100,000 for the year, the company *loses* $200,000. How? Well, what if the company's latest design—reflective neon thongs—was a bust and inventory piled up at the factory? Brooke's Bikinis would have suffered a sales decrease of 5 percent. Meanwhile, expenses increased somewhat due to stepped-up marketing to get rid of the thongs. Result: a loss of $200,000. The stock price of Brooke's Bikinis drops because the company lost money. Even though sales didn't drop by a lot, the earnings made the difference. Sometimes earnings drop even when sales rise. A company may be selling a lot of products, but it is spending more than it's making. Maybe raw material prices went up and the company couldn't pass on the increase to consumers. Remember what Mom used to say? Don't marry a guy who makes a lot of money but spends it all. Better pick someone who may not earn as much but knows how to save. *Remember, earnings are what counts. It's a major driver of stock prices.*

Using EPS to Pick Stocks

EPS? You mean you have to be a psychic to pick stocks? No, not ESP. It's EPS—Earnings Per Share. You've just learned about earnings and you already know about shares. Put the two together and you've got EPS—the company's earnings divided by the number of shares. *It's a way of looking at how much money a shareholder would get if the profit was divided.* If people at your office won a $1 million Lotto, the after-tax profit would be around $500,000. If five people chipped in to buy tickets, each would get $100,000. Earnings per share works the same way.

Finally, Brooke's Bikinis has recovered from the "Thong Fiasco." Business is back on track, thanks to sales of a new skirted bottom that flatters full figures. Profits are $100,000 for the year. But the company's investors want to know what their share of the profits will be. Take the earnings of $100,000 and divide by the company's 1 million outstanding shares. It comes to ten cents— the company made ten cents for each share an investor held. A shareholder with 1,000 shares could get $100, not counting the value of the stock itself.

But investors usually don't get all that money. A company doesn't have to give its profits to shareholders. It could give some and hold the rest, or keep everything to put back into the business. A profit distribution is called a *dividend*. Whatever the company chooses to do, the EPS serves one important purpose: *It tells you how well business is doing*. If EPS is going up, there's more money being made so business is getting better. If it's the other way around—business is weakening.

You will find two EPS figures: Basic and diluted. We want to use diluted EPS because they take into account all of the things that could chip away at the bottom line, such as dividends and the like. Diluted is akin to your take-home pay; your employer has taken out social security payments, the monthly health insurance cost, your work, contribution and other sundry. It's what's truly left to you—or a company.

Sometimes the EPS can be misleading. How? Well, let's say a company sells one of its divisions. If the company added the money received from the sale of an asset to its profits, the EPS would go up, but business hasn't really improved. The company just sold an asset and padded its profits. Read the earnings report of the company you're interested in to find out if some special event affected the EPS.

An Earnings Per Share report for XYZ Company might look something like this:

	1996	1997	1998	1999
Undiluted EPS	.43	.83	1.50	1.75
Diluted EPS	.41	.80	1.47	1.72

Let's go back to Brooke. She's a nervous lady. Brooke just worries about everything. When she leaves the house, she gets upset if she can't remember whether or not she turned off the stove. Did she? Didn't she? Then she dashes back home to find everything in order. When it comes to her bikini business, she worries too. Brooke doesn't want to wait until the year is over to discover how well her company is doing. Her accountant goes over the company's books four times a year—every three months, or quarterly—and reports the findings to company shareholders.

Other company presidents may not be as nervous, but all publicly held U.S. firms are required to report their business results by the quarter, just like Brooke's Bikinis. After every three months the company issues a "report card" of their business to investors. After all, shareholders have a right to know how well the company is doing. In Wall Street language, this report card is known as a *quarterly report*. It is also called a *10-Q*, since this is the form the government requires companies to file for their quarterly reports.

At the end of the year the company adds up earnings of all four quarters. This becomes the annual EPS (four quarters make a year). It is found in a report called a *10-K*. Expect five earnings-per-share numbers from a company yearly: four quarterly and an annual EPS.

Note: A company's year, also called its fiscal year, will not always start on January 1 and end on December 31. It can begin and end at any time—perhaps on May 1 until April 30 of the following year. The company will always identify its first, second, third, and fourth quarters and its fiscal year.

Now that you know what earnings per share means, what do you do with it? Find out whether EPS is growing by 25 percent or more. We'll tackle quarterly EPS first, and then the annual.

Step 1: Get the company's latest quarterly report from Standard & Poor's, Value Line, or online. Find the earnings per share for that quarter.

Step 2: Compare that EPS to the EPS from the same quarter *one year earlier.*

For example, if in the third quarter of the year 2000 the company had an EPS of twenty cents, you want to compare it to the third quarter of 1999, which had earnings per share of ten cents. *Remember: same time, last year.* We have to compare the same periods of different years—first with first, second with second, etc. Please don't mix your quarters. It can be misleading.

Let's say little Katie works hard at her homework throughout the school year, but during summer vacation she goes to camp and plays with her friends. Is it fair to compare the work she has done in the spring with summer? If you do, you'll come up with the wrong conclusion: "Oh no! Katie is slacking off! She wrote ten reports for school in the spring but none during summer!" That's a wrong conclusion.

Companies, especially retailers, essentially go through seasons as well. Do you think Macy's quarterly sales during the Christmas season will be the same as the spring quarter? No. It's much busier during the holidays. To get a valid comparison, you have to compare similar time periods.

Step 3: Do it again. Find an earlier quarter and compare it with the same quarter in a previous year.

If the latest quarter was the third quarter 2000, then an earlier quarter would be the second quarter 2000. Compare the earlier quarter's EPS with the EPS of the same quarter one year earlier. In our example, it would be the second quarter of 2000 versus the second quarter of 1999.

Repeat. Pick an even earlier quarter. In this case, it would be the first quarter of 2000. Compare it to the like period a year ago—first quarter of 1999.

Step 4: You've got six EPS figures. It's time to organize them. Match the same quarters together (for example, third with third, second with second) and clearly label to which years they belong. It should look something like this:

Third Qtr.		Second Qtr.		First Qtr.	
2000	**1999**	**2000**	**1999**	**2000**	**1999**
.20	.10	.15	.08	.09	.06

Step 5: Ask yourself, "Is the EPS rising in each pair of quarters?" In our example, third quarter 1999 had earnings of ten cents. But one year later the company earned twenty cents. What about the second quarter? It was eight cents in 1999 and fifteen cents in 2000. In the first quarter, we've got six cents in one year and nine cents the next. Earnings are up. So far so good. If earnings weren't increasing, you would throw out this candidate and find another company.

Step 6: Figure out the *earnings growth rate.* You're looking for an increase of at least 25 percent.

Let's look at the third quarters. Here, the figures are twenty cents and ten cents. Get out your calculator. Take the newer number (twenty cents) and subtract the older number (ten cents) from it. Twenty cents is punched in as ".20" and ten cents is ".10." After you subtract the two, the calculator should show this figure: ".10."

Now press the divide button and enter the *old* number (.10). The result should show "1." Press the multiply button and key in 100. The result is "100" or 100 percent. Repeating for the second-quarter numbers, you get 88 percent. The first quarter shows an increase of 50 percent.

Are earnings growing by more than 25 percent? You bet.

Step 7: It's time to look at annual earnings per share. As I said before, this is the EPS for all four quarters added together. From the stock reports, get the EPS for the last three to five years and compare each year's figure to the previous year. In every case, EPS must have grown by at least 25 percent.

BROOKE'S BIKINIS FOR BIG BEAUTIFUL WOMEN

Years 2000/1999	Years 1999/1998	Years 1998/1997	Years 1997/1996	Years 1996/1995
.55 .36	.36 .25	.25 .18	.18 .13	.13 .10
53%	44%	39%	38%	30%

Brooke's Bikinis passes the test

Extra Research: Other sources, such as www.marketguide.com, may show earnings in terms of their ranking too. In an EPS ranking, a stock is thrown in a bucket with all other U.S.-traded stocks and their earnings records are compared. Why do you need to compare your stock with others? If your company's earnings grew by an average of 25 percent, that may sound impressive, but not if most other companies are growing by at least 35 percent. Therefore, we want to know whether your stock compares favorably with others. We want your stock to have an EPS rank of 85 or higher. That means the company's earnings grew faster than at least 85 percent of all other public companies.

If your stock meets our earnings standards, check "E."

A Is for Atmosphere

When we invest, it's important to have the right market atmosphere. Remember the bull's-eye in Chapter 3? The outermost ring was the market. We should only invest when the market is in an uptrend. Otherwise, investing will be fraught with peril. Let's go over the stock market in more detail.

To measure the health of the market, we have to determine where the money is going—are there more buyers than sellers, or vice versa? But it's not easy to gauge a marketplace where millions of shares are being bought and sold every day. It's just too big. Wall Street thought so too. Thus it devised special measuring tools. These are called the *market indices*.

When you make soup, how do you know if there's enough salt? You don't slurp down the whole pot, you take a small sip. Market indices are like these little sips. By looking at a small part of the market, you'll know how the whole is doing.

The most famous index is the Dow Jones Industrial Average. It is the oldest market index, dating back to 1896. Today, the Dow is composed of thirty leading stocks on the New York Stock Exchange from a variety of industries that represent the U.S. economy. By looking at these companies, the rationale goes, we will get a sense of how the whole stock market is doing. Over the years the members of the Dow have changed. Only one company, General Electric, has stayed with the Dow since its inception.

The index is calculated every day and its results are plotted on a graph. Its result is expressed in points. If the Dow rises by one hundred, it means the market's up by one hundred points. This index is price-weighted, which means that the stocks with the highest prices have the most impact on the index. Therefore one high-priced stock, such as IBM or Hewlett-Packard, can drastically change the end result of the Dow on a given day.

The evening news always reports the Dow's swings. It may be up 55.75 points one day and down 13.35 points the next. After watching it for a while, you'll figure out what's a big move for the

Dow. Historically, the Dow has been regarded as a benchmark of the whole stock market. If the Dow is doing well, so is the market, the theory goes. But its status is waning. After all, it's only a measure of thirty stocks and they're all large-caps as well. How can that represent the whole market?

These days, Wall Street prefers the Standard & Poor's 500 over the Dow. Quick question. How many companies make up the S&P 500? "Let me see, five-hundred?" Right! The S&P comprises five-hundred leading companies in top industries—four-hundred industrial companies, forty financial firms, and sixty utility and transportation businesses. As such, it's a broader—and better—measure of the market, since it includes both large- and mid-caps. Unlike the Dow, the Standard & Poor's 500 Index is not price-weighted. Instead, it is weighted according to the market value of each company. Recall that market value is the price a company would fetch in the open market. Another word for it is *market cap*. Therefore, larger and more valuable companies affect the index more than its less-muscled brethren.

The third most popular yardstick is the NASDAQ Composite Index, which comprises more than 5,400 stocks. Like the S&P 500, this index is also weighted according to market cap; larger companies exert a heavier weight on the index. Unlike the Dow and S&P 500, NASDAQ contains large-, mid-, and small-caps. However, it is limited to companies that trade on the NASDAQ market, ignoring well-known established companies on the NYSE.

Even though the movements of these indices make the news, don't panic if you see a widespread decline. While many stocks would probably drop as well, it doesn't necessarily mean that yours will. Indices give you an idea of how well the market is performing *in general*. Your stock could be going the opposite direction of the market. Let's say the Dow dropped by 76.03 points one day but your Costco stock went up by three-quarters to 79½. That's normal; it happens all the time.

The Dow, S&P 500, and NASDAQ Composite aren't the only indices around. There are ones for mid-caps, small-caps, the whole U.S. market, international stocks, and bonds. The list goes on. But we'll focus on these three as indicators of how the stock market is doing in general.

Look at charts of the Dow, S&P 500, and NASDAQ. *If all three show lines that are going up, it means the market is on an up trend.* Put a check under "A." If the lines don't agree, follow the S&P 500's lead. Historically, the Dow and the NASDAQ eventually follow it.

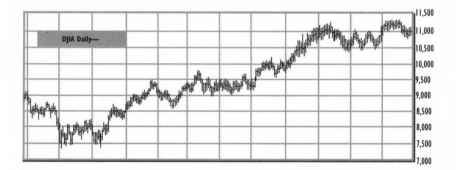

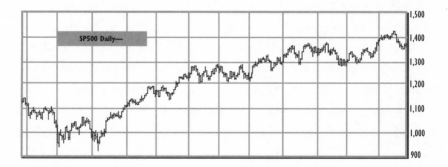

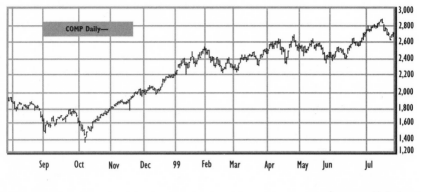

Source: www.bigcharts.com

P Is for P/E

How do you know if a stock is a good value? A popular way to measure it is with the P/E, or price-to-earnings ratio. The P/E is derived by dividing the stock's price by its past earnings in the last twelve months. Don't worry—you don't have to figure it out. Stock tables and company reports usually list it. But for the sake of understanding, I'll show you how to calculate it.

If a stock is priced at $30 a share and its earnings over the past year were $2, its P/E is 15, ($30 divided by $2). But what does the P/E really mean to you? In our example, if the company continues to make the same level of earnings, it will take *fifteen years* for you to recoup your $30 a share from the company's earnings. Let's say another stock is selling for $40, its earnings are $1 a share, therefore its P/E is 40. It will take *forty years* to get back the equivalent of your investment.

However, if a third stock you've got your eye on is selling for $100 but its earnings are $10 a share, this is the best value of all: Its P/E is 10. Best value? But it costs $100 a share while the other two cost $30 and $40! Yes, but it will only take ten years to recoup your investment on the $100 stock versus fifteen years and forty years for the others.

Think of it as buying a $125 dress from Bloomingdale's or a $35 dress at Betty's Bargains. The outfit procured from Betty's might seem like a better deal, but it is probably made from cheaper materials and could lose its shape and color in six months. However, the $125 dress may be more expensive at first, but if it lasts ten years, the garment effectively cost you $12.50 a year. Betty's bargain dress cost you $35 in less than a year.

Therefore, a high-priced stock may be a better value than a cheaper one, depending on how many years it will take to recoup an investment. Now, nobody expects to wait that long for a stock to theoretically return the money, so an investor wants a company to accelerate earnings at a faster rate so the investment will be recouped more quickly. That's why people are willing to pay a higher price for a faster-growing company.

Next, find the P/E for your stock's industry. If you're buying Exxon Mobil stock, you are looking for the oil industry. Compare Exxon Mobil's P/E with that of its industry. All else being equal, we want stocks that are trading at a lower P/E than their industries. Therefore, if the oil industry has an 18 P/E, we want to buy Exxon Mobil when its P/E is less than 18. We want good quality stocks, but we want to buy them on sale. Remember our two dresses? No doubt, the Bloomingdale's garment is of better quality. That's the one we want. But do we have to buy it at $125? Not if we can find the same dress on the sales rack marked down by 40 percent.

Another reason why you should prefer lower P/E stocks: When the market takes a tumble, expensive stocks always get hit the hardest. If investors think the market is going south, they will sell the high-P/E stocks first because they have less confidence the price will rise much further in a bad market.

If your stock has a lower P/E than its industry, put a check under "P."

(Note: After extolling the virtues of lower P/Es, don't get upset if I say something that will seem completely contradictory: Do not automatically disregard high-P/E stocks. Investing is not an exact science. If it were, we would all be rich by now. Investing is an art. When you see a stock with a higher P/E, take note of it but also look at its other characteristics. Try to get a feel for the company as a whole. If you believe its prospects justify a higher P/E, you might consider buying it. One of the best growth companies of our time has been Microsoft, and it has a high P/E. Most recently, it was 100.)

R Is for Return on Equity

When you invest your money in a company, wouldn't you want management to take care of it well? Of course. That's what return on equity, or ROE, measures. The equity here refers to shareholders' equity. It is money invested directly into a company plus any profits that were put back into the business. You can find the ROE figure in stock reports. However, if you want to know how ROE is derived, divide net income by shareholders' equity. If a company makes $300,000 and records shareholder equity of $2 million, the ROE is 15 percent. That's a good return on equity; a figure below 10 percent is weak. Warren Buffett, America's most famous billionaire investor and one of the world's richest men, requires his stocks to have at least a 12 percent ROE. *We'll aim for 15 and above.*

If your stock's ROE meets standards, put a check under "R."

O Is for Outstanding Performer

It makes sense that we should choose a stock that's an outstanding performer. But in what sense? In price. Its price has to have increased higher and faster than others. Wait a minute, you say. Don't we want to buy stocks at a good value? Wasn't that what P/E was all about? That's right, we do. But a stock that is setting price records doesn't necessarily have to be a high P/E company as well.

We want a stock whose price has appreciated more than most other stocks in the past year. It means investors like the company and are buying shares in droves. We measure this price performance in terms of rank. In a ranking, a stock's price is compared with others in its industry. Then the price performance of the industry itself is compared with other industries.

At www.marketguide.com, you'll get a price-performance table for each company. It should look something like this:

PRICE PERFORMANCE

Period	Actual (%)	vs. S&P 500(%)	Rank in Industry	Industry Rank
4 Week	31.9	25.4	77	98
13 Week	100.6	88.3	90	94
26 Week	422.6	349.3	99	96
52 Week	447.4	359.9	97	90
YTD	510.8	432.6	98	95

Note: Rank is a Percentile that Ranges from 0 to 99, with 99 = Best

Source: www.marketguide.com

© Market Guide Inc. 2000

Under "Rank in Industry" for the fifty-two-week period, we see a 97 rating. That's excellent. We're aiming for an 80 or higher rating, meaning the stock's price has outperformed 80 percent of all other companies in its industry.

Now let's go to the "Industry Rank" column. At the fifty-two-week level, we also want to see an 80 or higher. In our sample chart, we see a 90 rank. This company passes standards!

When you see a high rating in both columns, it means you have a hot stock in an industry that's sizzling.

If the stock you're contemplating buying has price rankings of 80 and higher, it gets a check mark under "O."

F Is for Float

No, not root beer. A *float* in Wall Street parlance means the number of shares available for the public to buy and sell. It is different from *authorized shares*—the number of shares the company asked a government agency, the Securities and Exchange Commission, to approve. It is also distinct from *outstanding shares*, which adds together the stock held by company insiders such as management and directors with shares available to the public. The float, therefore, is outstanding shares minus the stock held by company insiders. You find this information in a company's stock report.

For example, a company might ask the SEC to authorize 50 million shares. It won't use 50 million all at once, but it is easier to get the bulk approved and sell them when needed because there is a lot of work involved in getting SEC approval. The company may issue 10 million shares—these are outstanding shares. Insiders of the company (people who have access to sensitive company information, such as management and directors) get the first chance to purchase stock from this pool. If insiders purchased 3 million shares, the public can buy the remaining 7 million shares. This is the float.

For our purposes, the smaller the float, the better. That means you bypass the IBMs of the world and zoom in on the up-and-coming small- and mid-caps *before* they become huge conglomerates. There's nothing wrong with big companies, but the stock prices of small companies tend to appreciate faster because of their smaller float. It's also easier for smaller firms to grow—double in size for instance—than for major companies to do so.

Over time the prices of smaller companies on average rise higher than large-caps. Did you know that $10,000 invested in Microsoft in 1987 is worth $1.75 million today? But the same amount invested in McDonald's would have yielded only $79,000? Back then, McDonald's was an established fast-food chain that eclipsed Microsoft. Wall Street had considered McDonald's four times more valuable than the software company. Today, Microsoft is worth six times more than the burger chain.

Why do companies with small floats tend to appreciate faster than larger-float stocks? It's the law of supply and demand: With a smaller float, there are fewer shares to buy. When demand rises, the bidding for the stock will drive its price higher than that of a company with plenty of shares.

Therefore, look for stocks with a float of 50 million or fewer. If your stock has a small float, put a check under "F."

I Is for Institutional Investors

Your twelve-year-old son, Kevin, gets the lead part in a school play. At the close of the production, you get tears in your eyes at what you feel is an absolutely brilliant performance by your son. That's a good endorsement. But wouldn't it be more significant for a Hollywood agent to have recognized his talents?

With stocks, you want a company that has been given the thumbs-up by the experts—institutional investors. They are the big boys and girls with lots of money: mutual funds, pension funds, insurance companies, bank trust departments, and others. They include the California Public Employees Retirement System, a behemoth pension fund, and Fidelity Magellan, America's largest mutual fund. If a small investor is a mouse, they're elephants.

We want a company that institutional investors also own. Companies show their institutional ownership in their stock reports. If the big players like the stock, it's usually a good endorsement.

However, we want some institutional presence but not too much: *Put a preference on companies where institutions hold less than 50 percent of its stock.* A higher rate of ownership means most of the shares have already been bought by institutional investors. Hence there's not as many stocks left for another institution to buy. Without more buying action in huge quantities, the price isn't going to appreciate strongly.

Which Way Is the Big Money Headed?

So your company has institutional ownership. But are they showing their optimism about the stock's future by buying more shares or have they realized they made a mistake and started to sell stock? Our next task is to see if institutions are on a buying spree or not. A stock that's being stockpiled is one that's *under accumulation.* When institutions are bailing out of a stock, it is *under distribution.*

You can find trading data on www.marketguide.com. The

three-month *net* purchases figure—which totals buys and sells—
should be a positive number. It means buys outnumbered sells.

INSTITUTIONAL OWNERSHIP

➤ % Shares Owned	26.98
# of Institutions	42
Total Shares Held (Mil)	1.786
➤ 3 Mo. Net Purchased (Mil)	0.291
3 Mo. Shares Purchased (Mil)	0.770
3 Mo. Shares Sold (Mil)	0.479

Source: www.marketguide.com

© Market guide Inc. 2000

In the chart above, we see that institutional investors own
26.98 percent of the shares. That's good. They hold some ownership, but there's room for more big investors to come in. The
"3 Mo. Net Purchased (Mil)" figure is 0.291. This is expressed in
millions; therefore, it would translate to 291,000 shares. Since it
is a positive number, we can assume that when you added up the
shares bought and sold, buyers came out ahead by 291,000 shares.
That's another positive sign—more buying than selling.

If you go to another source for institutional trading information, it may not tell you how many actual net shares there were in
the past three months. Instead, other reports might express it in
percentages. They will show you the percent of shares owned by
institutions in the most recent quarter compared with the previous
quarter. In this case, look for an increase in the percentage ownership. It means the heavyweights are buying.

If net purchases are positive, or if institutional ownership is
increasing, put a check under "I."

T Is for Top Dollar

So far, your stock candidate looks good. But should we buy it now? You can tell with a quick glance: Is the stock at or within 10 percent of its fifty-two-week high? If so, it might be the right time to jump in, but we'll know for sure when we go over stock charts in Chapter 5. Buying when the stock price is high is one of the most difficult rules to follow. We love sales! But don't get fooled into believing that because the price is cheap you're necessarily getting a bargain. Remember, you get what you pay for. If a stock hits a new fifty-two-week low, there must be a reason why investors are bailing out and it's not good news. So stick with the winners.

Let's Rewind and Play It Again

Look for the following characteristics in stocks, using the acronym "BE A PROFIT."

Beta: The higher the beta, the more wildly a company's stock price will swing. The risks are greater, but so are rewards. When faced with two good candidates, the stock with the lower beta will help you sleep better at night. However, you're also forgoing the possibility of greater riches.

Earnings per share: Another word for profits. It is the best indication of a company's health. Compare the most recent quarter with the same quarter of the previous year, then go back two more quarters. Compare annual EPS going back three to five years. Earnings should be growing by at least 25 percent.

Atmosphere: The market must show an uptrend. Check charts for the Dow Jones Industrial Average, Standard & Poor's 500, and the NASDAQ Composite Index. They should all be heading up. If they don't all agree in direction, follow the S&P 500.

P/E ratio: The price-to-earnings multiple measures a stock's expensiveness in relation to its profits. Look up a stock's P/E and make sure it is lower than the industry's.

Return on Equity: ROE measures how well management takes care of investors' money. If the company is turning out a high profit for every dollar you have entrusted them, you know you are betting on a good contender. We want 15 percent or higher.

Outstanding performance: A good stock is one that is in demand. Hence its stock price will be rising. We are seeking a price rank of at least 80 in two areas: a stock within its industry and the industry compared with other industries. Therefore, we can be assured that it's a hot stock in a sizzling industry.

Float: Look for companies with a float of 50 million or fewer shares. We want smaller companies because they grow much faster than large corporations.

Institutional investors: Follow the big money. Look for companies owned by institutional investors. But make sure institutions don't hold more than 50 percent of shares. In addition, institutions should be increasing their ownership.

Top dollar: Choose companies that have recently hit their fifty-two-week high. History shows that once a stock sets a new record, it will go on to higher ground.

Let's Put It All Together

Let's go through "BE A PROFIT" together, shall we? Let's imagine that you have bravely skipped that afternoon cup of steaming Starbucks for the past six months now, risking caffeine withdrawal in order to save money for stocks. Emptying the cookie tin where you stashed your cash, you count the greenbacks in your hand. Five hundred dollars. You have reached your goal.

Running to your computer, you turn it on to start a journey that is long overdue: buying stocks. You know that it's a good time to invest since the market is on an uptrend. You made sure to check that day's *Wall Street Journal*.

Logging on to www.marketguide.com, you search for hot industries. Clicking on "What's Hot?" you're faced with "Hottest Sectors" and "Hottest Industries." Going to "Hottest Sectors," you get a list. Which one should you choose? What about services? It seems to be doing well—not only have the stock prices of its companies increased more than that of other industries, its earnings and sales are also healthy. Clicking on "Services," you get a list of industries. You try retail/apparel. Profits and revenues are robust and you're a shopping expert, after all. Digging a little deeper, you browse the list of companies within the retail/apparel industry. A name stands out: Bebe Stores Inc. Not only are its earnings impressive, you actually know this company. You remember seeing their store at the mall. It always seems busy. Clicking on "Bebe," you start reading the company's profile. Bebe designs contemporary clothing for women, targeting hip females from ages eighteen to thirty-five. Its clothes have been worn on *Ally McBeal* and *Melrose Place*. Looks good. Let's put it through BE A PROFIT.

You write out your checklist:

Co. name	B	E	A	P	R	O	F	I	T
BEBE									

You can start with any letter, but let's go for earnings. The www.marketguide.com Web site contains EPS figures, but wall streetcity.com lays it out more conveniently for us. Go to the other site and type in Bebe's stock symbol—which you know is BEBE from the company profile you read. Choose "Quarterly Earnings" in the selection box. You will see this:

QUARTERLY EARNINGS TABLE—
Last Eight Calendar Quarters

This years EPS		Last Years EPS		% Change
Q1 99	(0.21)	Q1 98	(0.14)	50.0%
Q4 98	0.38	Q4 97	0.23	65.2%
Q3 98	0.21	Q3 97	0.16	31.2%
Q2 98	0.20	Q2 97	0.08	150.0%

The first quarter of 1999 had an earnings per share of twenty-one cents while the first quarter of 1998 had fourteen cents. By how much did earnings go up? Look in the "% Change" column. It shows a 50 percent increase. Great! For the fourth quarter of 1999 and 1998, we see an EPS increase of 65 percent. In the third quarters of 1999 and 1998, EPS grew by 31 percent.

To get the yearly EPS, go back to www.marketguide.com. In the box for the stock quotes, type in BEBE. The company's snapshot should come up. On the left side, click on "highlights." It will tell you the three- and five-year EPS growth rate. Bebe's annual EPS averaged 44.49 percent for three years and 109.71 percent for five years. Therefore, the retailer meets our earnings standards of at least 25 percent.

E for earnings gets a check mark.

Now click the snapshot link to the left, to go back to Bebe's company profile. You'll come across this nifty report:

KEY RATIOS & STATISTICS
(as of July 28, 1999)

Price & Volume		Valuation Ratios	
Recent Price $	31.75	Price/Earnings (TTM)	31.85
52 Week High $	50.00	Price/Sales (TTM)	4.31
52 Week Low $	10.00	Price/Book (MRQ)	11.06
Avg Daily Vol (Mil)	0.20	Price/Cash Flow (TTM)	28.60
Beta	NA		

Share Related Items		Per Share Data	
Mkt. Cap (Mil) $	768.26	Earnings (TTM) $	1.00
Shares Out (Mil)	24.20	Sales (TTM) $	7.36
Float (Mil)	2.40	Book Value (MRQ) $	2.87
		Cash Flow (TTM) $	1.11

Source: www.marketguide.com
© Market Guide Inc. 2000

Look at the company's price. Is it within 10 percent of its fifty-two-week high? No. Even if everything else about the stock meets our standards, this tells us that it's not the time to buy. Put an X under "T," which stands for top dollar.

B is for beta. Unfortunately, the company's too young to have a beta. But if you look at its price fluctuations for the past year, you'll see that the stock soared from $10 to $50—a five-fold percent increase! Recall that beta is how wildly a stock price swings compared with the market. In Bebe's case, the beta should be high, but it's acceptable because we're going to be a little more aggressive.

Glancing down to "Share Related Items" under company snapshot, you'll see the float. Bebe has a float of 2.4 million shares, well under our 50 million threshold. Check "F."

Here's one more trick. Let's find out how many shares the insiders own. Take outstanding shares—24.2 million—and subtract the 2.4 million float. You'll end up with 21.8 million shares. That means Bebe is heavily owned by insiders. That's good! It means management and directors will take good care of the company since they own most of the shares.

On the same Web site, click on "Performance." Here, you'll find the stock's price performance and institutional ownership.

PRICE PERFORMANCE
(as of July 28, 1999)

Period	Actual (%)	vs. S&P 500 (%)	Rank In Industry	Industry Rank
4 Week	17.1	13.5	88	22
13 Week	−17.5	−17.5	25	36
26 Week	−15.9	−24.1	21	67
52 Week	101.6	69.5	95	91
YTD	−10.2	−18.7	26	82

Note: Rank is a Percentile that Ranges from 0 to 99, with 99 = Best

(continued on following page)

Institutional Ownership		Insider Trading (Prev. 6 Months)	
% Shares Owned	13.88	Net Insider Trades	−5
# of Institutions	56	# Buy Transactions	0
Total Shares Held (Mil)	3.358	# Sell Transactions	5
3 Mo. Net Purchases (Mil)	0.726	Net Shares Purchased (Mil)	−0.075
3 Mo. Shares Purchased (Mil)	1.921	# Shares Purchased (Mil)	0.000
3 Mo. Shares Sold (Mil)	1.195	# Shares Sold (Mil)	0.075

Source: www.marketguide.com/Vickers Institutional Research

© Market Guide Inc. 2000

Isn't this company outstanding? Under "Rank in Industry," Bebe has a 95 rating for the last fifty-two weeks. That means its price has gone up higher than 95 percent of all other public companies in its industry. The "Industry Rank" is 91, telling us that it's a hot industry. Both beat our 80 or higher standard.

Put a check under "O."

Under "Institutional Ownership," we see that Bebe is held by fifty-six institutions that collectively own 13.88 percent of the company's outstanding shares. There's certainly more room for other big investors. Glance down to the "3 Mo. Net Purchases" column. We see that it's a positive number. Since the figure is expressed in millions, the table tells us that shares purchased outnumbered shares sold by 726,000 shares. "I" gets a check.

Finally, let's click on "Comparison." You'll see several tables, but pay attention to these two:

RATIO COMPARISON

(as of July 28, 1999)

Valuation Ratios	Company	Industry	Sector	S&P 500
P/E Ratio (TTM)	31.85	32.56	33.34	35.90
P/E High—Last 5 Years	NA	50.43	42.12	44.67
P/E Low—Last 5 Years	NA	11.86	15.18	14.67
Beta	NA	1.01	0.91	1.00
Price to Sales (TTM)	4.31	2.89	4.69	5.46
Price to Book (MRQ)	11.06	16.14	6.57	8.96
Price to Tangible Book	11.06	17.53	8.48	11.65
Price to Cash Flow (TTM)	28.60	23.60	26.77	28.79
Price to Free Cash Flow	48.40	67.00	50.40	45.24
% Owed by Institutions	13.88	58.25	51.20	62.56

Management Effect. (%)	Company	Industry	Sector	S&P 500
Return on Assets (TTM)	34.88	24.40	5.14	8.91
Return on Assets—5 Yr Avg.	NA	16.40	4.81	8.35
Return on Investment	47.16	37.45	7.98	14.18
Return on Invest.—5 Yr. Avg.	NA	25.09	7.71	13.22
Return on Equity (TTM)	49.51	53.03	16.02	23.64
Return on Equity—5 Yr. Avg.	NA	29.82	14.92	21.80

Bebe's price-to-earnings ratio is 31.85, which is less than the industry's 32.56 and the sector's 33.34. Bebe is considered to be a good value at the moment. Put a check under "P." But before you rush out to buy this one on sale, dig deeper to see if bad news is keeping the stock lower or we have indeed discovered a good bargain.

What about return on equity, the "R" in our system? For Bebe, it is 49.51, which is slightly less than the industry but much higher than the sector. The company's ROE more than meets our standard of 15. Put a check market under "R."

Now What?

We conclude that Bebe is a possible buy. Believe it or not, you've just learned what Wall Street calls *fundamental analysis*. Fundamental analysis assesses a company's strengths and prospects through a critical examination of its business. It looks at the company itself and largely disregards the opinions of most investors. It doesn't care what they think about the company.

But we *should* care. How other investors regard a stock is important. After all, they are the buyers and sellers. If I have a great product but nobody wants to buy it, what good is it? Therefore, we have to find out what other people think. That's where *technical analysis* comes in. In the next chapter, I'll teach you how to decipher stock charts to see what the investing public is up to. We'll also look at stock-price patterns that have repeated throughout history. Our purpose is to know when to jump into a stock since timing is critical.

You could spot a promising company, but if you don't buy it at the right time, you are doomed to fail. Choosing the right stock is half the battle, but buying it at the right time is what eventually wins the war.

CHAPTER FIVE

Taking the Plunge

It was the sale of the century. Everything in the store was 70 percent off—Jones New York, Donna Karan, Calvin Klein, and Liz Claiborne, to name a few designers whose clothes you'd brave shark-infested waters to buy. But you will have to be quick to get the best of the bunch. It's five minutes before the store opens and you're outside with a group of other veteran shoppers. Some are doing leg stretches as they prepare to storm the gates.

As a salesman starts to unlock the store's main doors, your legs tense a little as they poise to sprint. Looking around, you see expectant, focused faces all around. It's going to be tough competition, but you're tougher. Crouching a bit so you can push against the pavement for an energetic spurt, you mentally do the countdown: three . . . two . . . one. You're off!

As an expert shopper, you know that timing is important. After all, why pay $250 for a suit when a week later you can get it for $125 on sale? When you invest, timing is even more critical. We may have our eye on a good stock, but until we get a sign to buy it at the right time, we won't do as well. In Chapter 4, we explored the tenets of fundamental analysis by scrutinizing a company's profits, prospects, and stock prices. Using BE A PROFIT, we narrowed down the list of candidates.

However, that was only half of the picture. We know what we want to buy, but when do we buy it? This is where *technical analysis* comes into the picture. With technical analysis, we'll learn to read the past and present movements of a stock's price to determine where the stock is headed. By knowing a stock's direction, we can better pinpoint a good time to jump in, just before the stock surges upward.

Fundamental analysis tells us what to buy and technical analysis shows us when to take the plunge.

Technical analysis begins with a stock chart, which is a graph of stock prices. This is what it looks like:

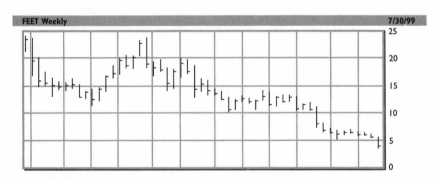

Source: www.bigcharts.com

The chart above is a *bar chart*. There are other types of charts such as the line and candlestick, but the most commonly used is the bar. We will use bar charts in this chapter.

A stock chart shows a stock's price as it changes over a period of time—it can be days, weeks, months, or years. There's even a chart for prices as they move within a day! This is called the *intraday* movement.

Now go back to the chart above. The zigzags tell us the path of the stock's price. It goes up, it goes down, it goes sideways. Take a closer look at the path itself and you'll see that it is made up of little bars with horizontal lines running across them. They look like this:

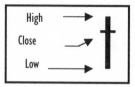

The top of the bar is the highest price reached by the stock during a given period of time. The bottom is the stock's lowest price and the dash in the middle is the price at which the stock ended. If you're using a daily chart, the top would be the highest price that stock traded at during the day and the bottom would be its lowest point. The dash tells you where the stock stopped trading when the day ended. If it's a weekly chart, the top of the bar would be the highest price attained by the stock that week, the bottom would be the lowest, and the dash tells you where the stock landed when trading ended for the week.

For most of this chapter, we're going to use weekly charts. I like these better because they show a longer trend.

Now let's move to the bottom half of a stock chart. This is what it looks like:

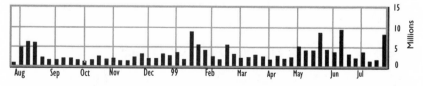

See towers that jut up like jagged piano keys? Since we're using a weekly chart, each tower represents the stock's volume for a certain week. Volume is the number of shares that are bought and sold.

The volume tells investors how popular a stock is at a given time. Like the volume light on your stereo, a tall volume bar in a stock chart tells us there's plenty of fuss going on: Many investors are buying and selling the stock. A short tower is just the opposite: ho-hum. There's not much action. Volume gives investors one of the most important clues for technical analysis. Our task is to find out what the volume is telling us.

Here is the top half of a weekly bar chart for MiniMed, Inc., a California company that makes insulin pumps and related accessories.

MNMD

High, Low, Close

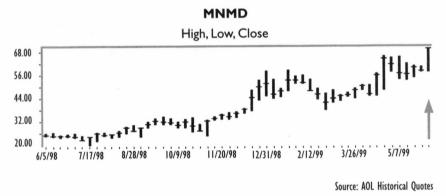

Source: AOL Historical Quotes

MiniMed closed with a bang the last week of the chart. The dash is right at the top of the vertical line, indicating that this stock closed at the high for the week, a very healthy sign.

One, Two, and Three: All Together Now

Let's practice reading the MiniMed stock chart. Start with the left side of the graph. These are stock prices. On the chart, they range from $20 to $68. Next, pick one bar and correspond it to the price on the left. Let's choose the one with the arrow. The stock went wild that day: It rose as high as around $70 a share and sank to as low as $56. MiniMed closed around $70. When did this happen? Look at the bottom of the graph for dates. Since it's a weekly chart, each notch on the graph represents a week. Counting by the week, we know that the bar above the arrow represents the week of June 4, 1999.

Let's read one more bar. What about the short one next to the bar we just read? That was the week of May 28, 1999. During that time MiniMed was a sleepy stock. It didn't go anywhere. The low of the week was around $56 and the high was about $59. (If you want to get exact figures, and you were able to get these charts online, some Web sites let you click on the bars for the information you need. For our purposes, it's not critical.)

A Few Observations

When a company's stock chart is composed mostly of short bars, it's a sign of a stable stock: the price doesn't plunge to deep valleys or rocket to staggering peaks like a death-defying roller coaster. The beta is moderate or low. You may prefer this type of stock if you dislike volatility.

However, some people thrive on risk. In the late 1990s, Internet stocks were popular among aggressive investors because of their wild price swings; it wasn't unusual to get a $20 rise or dip on a $150 stock. Betting on such volatility could enrich—or impoverish—investors overnight.

When a stock's price closes in the top half of its bar or range, it's also a good sign. In the price tug-of-war between buyers and sellers, buyers must have won.

Crank Up the Volume

Now let us look at a volume graph or chart. It is the stock
chart's handy partner.

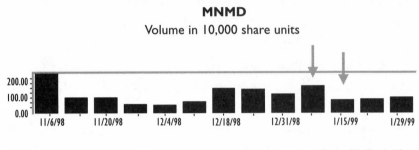

MNMD
Volume in 10,000 share units

The left side of the volume graph lists the number of shares:
"0," "100," and "200." Wait a minute. You mean only one hundred
or two hundred shares were traded in a week? That seems too
small. Good observation! The top of the chart gives us a clue about
how many actual shares exchanged hands. It says "MNMD—Volume in 10,000 share units." That means whatever number we see,
we still have to add four zeroes to it. Therefore 100 is really 1
million shares and 200 should be read as 2 million shares.

Let's practice reading the volume graph. For the week of January 8, 1999—it's the tower between December 31, 1998, and
January 15, 1999—approximately 1.7 million MiniMed shares exchanged hands. The following week, volume was cut in half to
822,000 shares.

It is time to read the stock and volume charts together. Here
is the chart for MNMD.

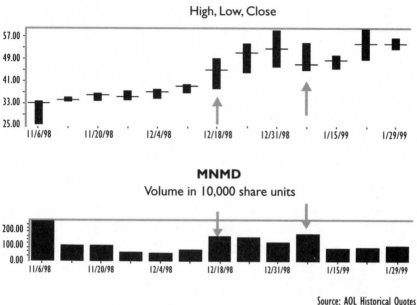

MNMD
High, Low, Close

MNMD
Volume in 10,000 share units

Source: AOL Historical Quotes

During the week of December 18, 1998, we see that MiniMed ranged from around $37 to $49 a share. It closed at about $45. Looking at the corresponding volume for the week, we see that more than 1.5 million shares were traded. In contrast, the stock had a volume of around only 700,000 shares in the prior week. The stock price didn't move much as well—ranging from $36 to $39 before closing at $38. What about January 8, 1999? It hit a high of around $55 and a low of $45 before closing at $47. The volume was also high at 1.7 million shares.

High Volume Means High Activity

Pay attention to high-volume towers. The volume graph may not be exciting, but it gives us important clues for successful investing. *Heavy volume together with a hefty price increase is a signifi-cant event.* It tells us that there is plenty of trading activity going on and buyers are outnumbering sellers. When you see a lot of volume, check the matching price bar on top. Is the closing price higher for that week than the previous week? If there's a noticeable increase, it's a positive development.

In MiniMed's case, such an event occurred on December 18. The price closed at $45 that week, much higher than the previous week. The volume corresponding to the bar is tall—more than 1.5 million shares compared with around 700,000 the week before.

Now look at the week of January 8, 1999. Volume for this week was 1.7 million shares and the closing price was $47. Sounds good. But when you check the price bar, get ready for some bad news. Volume was higher, but the $47 closing is *lower* than last week's $52. This is a troubling sign because sellers are outnumbering buyers. Investors are selling off the stock.

Remember: Heavy volume is a signal. When it is accompanied by a price increase, investors are buying up the stock. When there's a price decline, investors are bailing out.

The Heavy Hitters Are Back

When volume rises sharply, it is due to a lot of shares being traded. But just who is behind this much activity? Small investors don't have that kind of buying power. Yes, you've got it: The institutional investors are back. Remember, they buy in large quantities. If a stock rises on heavy volume, it means the institutions are buying. If the price sinks, they are selling.

What if volume is light? What's happening? Most of the big buyers are staying out of the stock; small investors are doing the trading. When you see a price rise or drop on light volume, it indicates that the big money is not actively involved. Thus it is not as significant. We want to watch the big players move.

To Bebe or Not to Bebe, That Is the Question

Now that you know how to spot significant volume increases, what do you do with this information? We will use it to tell us when to buy and sell a stock.

Remember Bebe stores from Chapter 4? We determined that we like the company's fundamentals. It has a good business model, earnings are strong, and institutions own part of the company. The only question we couldn't answer was when to buy the stock.

Technical analysis can help. First, let's take a look at Bebe's weekly chart.

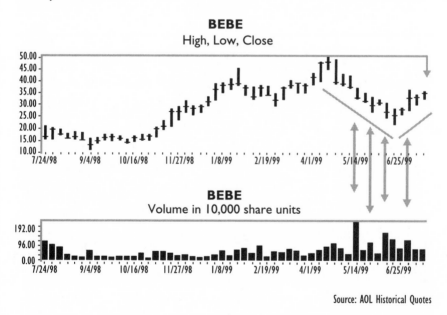

BEBE
High, Low, Close

BEBE
Volume in 10,000 share units

Source: AOL Historical Quotes

From mid-May to mid-June, you see heavy volume increases in four specific weeks. These are the towers highlighted by arrows.

You've already learned that high-volume increases are signals. What is each tower telling us? The first heavy volume week occurred on May 14, 1999. Looking at the corresponding price bar, you notice that the stock has dropped from the previous week. That's a bad sign. For us, it's not the time to buy. We're waiting for a heavy volume day with a price increase.

Some people might jump aboard while Bebe keeps dropping, thinking to get the stock on sale. If they do, they will be sorry.

The second heavy volume week happened during May 28, 1999. Time to buy Bebe? Not yet. The price dropped again from the past week. It's the same story for the third volume tower as well. By this time the bargain hunters are probably getting nervous. Bebe keeps heading down! The ones who cannot take the ride will be tempted to sell at a loss.

The fourth tower is where it gets interesting.

Bebe's volume rose to 1 million shares during the week of July 2, 1999—a significant increase from trading of 800,000 shares the week before. It's an encouraging sign, but we should wait until Bebe is within 10 percent of its fifty-two-week high (see the lone arrow on top of the chart) before we buy.

To understand why, let's go into the mind of an investor. Call him Uncle Louie. In April, Uncle Louie sees Bebe's stock rise like the hemlines of the skirts it sells. Smelling a quick profit, he hurriedly buys the stock without doing much research. He gets in during the week of April 15, when the stock hit its fifty-two-week high of about $46 a share. However, instead of seeing his fortunes rise, Bebe started heading down.

At first, Uncle Louie didn't panic. It's going to turn around soon, he told himself. It is a good company with healthy earnings. A few more weeks, and he'll be rich! So he waits.

April ends. May comes around and Bebe is still intent on going down. Uncle Louie starts to sweat. What's happening? His sure thing is uncertain! He wants to get out, but he can't make himself take the loss. While he wrings his hands in indecision, June comes around. Bebe is still languishing. By this time Uncle Louie has given up on the stock. He won't sell it yet because he doesn't want to take the loss, but he will sniff around for another company to make him rich.

Uncle Louie is part of what's called the *overhead supply*. This is a group of investors who buy at a high and suddenly see their stock dropping. Typically, they will hold on to the stock until they can break even on it. That's why you don't want to buy the stock during May and June. The price has not yet reached the break-even point for the overhead supply. As soon as the price hits the level at which they purchased, there could be a heavy downwind coming our way from these sellers and this wave could prevent the stock from continuing upward. It's not a good idea to get caught in this. However, if Bebe's uptrend is powerful enough, it will continue its ascent despite Uncle Louie and his ilk dumping the stock. When high volume occurs on a day with a hefty price increase, that's when we buy.

Therefore the answer to our question of "To Bebe, or not to Bebe?" is no, we should not buy it yet. But we should wait for a buying opportunity.

Mom's Eagle Eye

When you were growing up, do you remember how hard it was to keep anything from your mother? Even your best trick—the distracting cough at the dinner table together with the quick drop of the broccoli to the floor for Rover—didn't fool dear old Mom. She just gave you a second helping of the green stuff. To this day, you don't even know how she finds things out about you. You're convinced she's got a super eagle eye.

You'll need those eagle eyes for our next lesson: spotting patterns in stock charts. Learn to pull back a bit and look at the chart as a whole, like you would an abstract painting. As prices are plotted on a chart, they begin to form patterns that prove to be significant over the years. These patterns may forewarn us of things to come in the price of our stock. Good investors pay close attention to these warnings.

At the most basic level, stocks go through three phases: *uptrend, downtrend, and basing.*

We can tell what stage a stock is in by drawing trend lines through the stock charts. You can draw trend lines by connecting the highs and lows of a stock's price, like this:

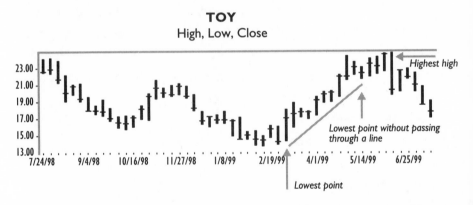

TOY
High, Low, Close

You may fancy yourself the next Picasso and start dreaming up creative ways to draw lines—maybe form mini-pyramids? I'm sorry to quash your artistic aspirations, but resist the temptation. The more wild you get, the less helpful your trend line will be. Remember, we are going to be making some pretty serious decisions based on the lines you are about to draw.

Our goal is to identify a stock's current trend and watch for instances when the line is breached. In an uptrend, the trend line points upward. But this line may be crossed when the stock drops precipitously. In a downtrend, the line may be broken when the stock rises sharply. In both cases, breaking the trend line signifies a change in direction for the stock. We investors can use this knowledge to our advantage. When we see a stock in an uptrend, we can buy in and ride it higher. Once we see the trend line broken, it might be time to sell. Conversely, we will observe a stock that is in a downtrend. Once the downward trend line is breached, we know the tide's turning. We can buy the stock and ride it up.

Make trend lines your ally. By using them correctly, you can make investment decisions using logic instead of emotion.

Let's look at the trends more closely.

Uptrend Phase

To draw trend lines in this phase, connect the stock's lowest low up to the point just before its highest high. Make sure not to draw through any price bars. Consider the following chart for Toys "R" Us:

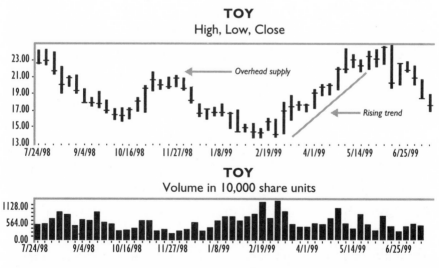

Source: AOL Historical Quotes

The rising trend is the line that the stock cannot seem to drift under, at least for the time being. At this point the trend line gets a new name too: It is also called the *support line*. Look at the Toys "R" Us chart again.

The sooner you identify the rising trend line, the longer your ride will be. This is called the growth phase. Still, there are no guarantees. These trends may end at any time.

Downtrend Phase

In drawing a downtrend, look for a period of downturn in a stock and draw a line connecting the highest point down to right before the lowest low without crossing through any price bars. It should look something like this:

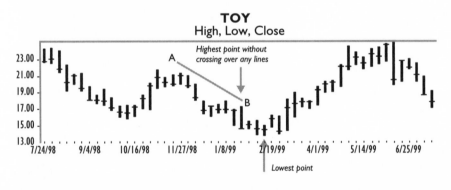

Source: AOL Historical Quotes

The party's over, for now. The growth phase has sputtered and it's time for the stock price to drop. Don't be alarmed; it's a normal phase for a stock. Unlike rising trend lines, falling trends are defined by declining lines that are drawn between two or more peaks. (See point A and B above.) The stock seems unable to break through the price at this line, whenever the stock attempts to cross it—buyers are pushing up the price—a wave of sellers come in and bring the price back down. This line is called the *resistance* line. Here is an example of Toys "R" Us during a falling trend:

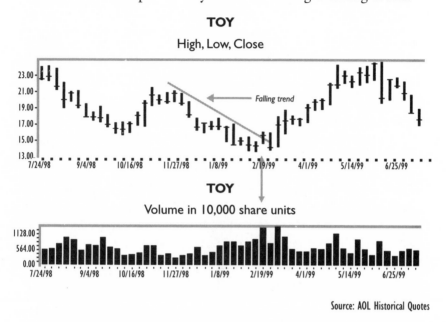

TOY

High, Low, Close

Falling trend

TOY

Volume in 10,000 share units

When you see a downtrend, extend the trend line a bit to see the point at which the stock will breach it. Then sit and watch. As it passes up through this line of resistance, look for heavy volume. You may be witnessing the birth of an uptrend.

Don't buy a stock that is caught in a downtrend. Watch for it to stop declining first. Once it reverses course, jump in when the volume doubles its thirty-day average *and* the price rises by 1 percent or more. The thirty-day average volume may be found in the stock tables of financial publications.

Toys "R" Us did just that on the week of February 19, 1999.

Basing Phase

In this phase, the stock can't make up its mind where to go, so it bounces around in a tight price range. There are no mountain ranges and no valleys. Just a dry, flat plain that stretches for at least seven weeks. But before you fall asleep, take note that even a flat base like this one can be profitable. Look for an upward breakout. That's when the stock price suddenly shows some life and shoots up. It has gone against the boring basing trend. Something's up with the company for investors to push its price up dramatically. The longer the basing phase, the more significant this break is.

An upward breakout is usually accompanied by heavy volume. Make sure the volume is twice as much as the thirty-day average and the stock price appreciates by at least 1 percent from the week before. *If volume and price increases support the breakout pattern, it's time to buy!* Don't worry if you've missed the buy point by a few days. If it's a true signal, the stock will continue to go up.

Here is an example of a basing pattern that turned sweet for those who were watching this stock closely.

NITE

High, Low, Close

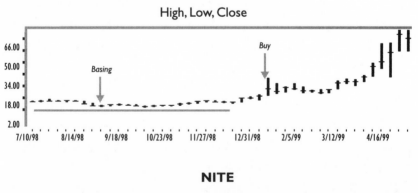

NITE

Volume in 10,000 share units

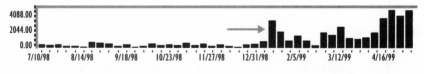

Source: AOL Historical Quotes

The Market Is Queen

It's important to treat the market with respect. The market is always right. Therefore, don't sell in the middle of an uptrend, because the stock will keep rising, and don't buy in the midst of a downtrend because the sky is still falling. Rather, watch for signs of the stock price changing course. That means you'll never buy at the exact bottom or sell at the stock's apex. But as long as you get on the gravy train quickly enough, you're a winner in the end.

Stock Patterns

We've gone over the three basic stages of a stock. It's time to look for stock patterns. What's the difference? A stock pattern forms an abstract picture rather than a straight up- or downtrend line. We're going to look over some patterns that have repeated themselves historically. Like trend lines, we can use stock patterns to our advantages. Once we identify a certain pattern emerging, we know that based on the past, the stock price is going to move in a certain direction. That knowledge will help us decide when to buy the stock profitably.

Some of these patterns' names are rather whimsical, but don't underestimate their importance. Grown-ups have made their fortunes with "cups with a handle" and "double bottoms."

Cup with a Handle

This is one of the healthiest stock patterns around. Cups with a handle are most often found at the beginning of a market move, usually after a painful correction or drop in the market. Don't expect to find many cups-with-handle patterns either during or at the end of a major market advance.

Here is a weekly bar chart for Associated Group, Inc., a wireless-communications-service company in Pittsburgh.

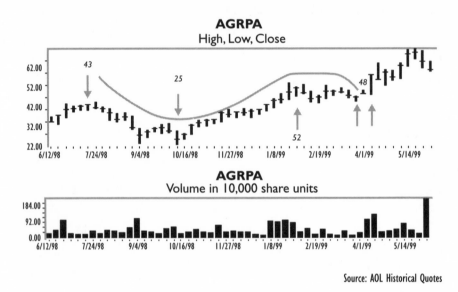

Source: AOL Historical Quotes

See how nicely the stock's movements form the rounded bottom of a cup and the smaller half-moon of a handle? It will be easier to visualize the pattern if you focus on the overall shape and not on each of the weekly fluctuations. When you spot a cup and a handle, it's time to get excited! But at what price should you buy? Take a closer look at our cup.

At the top left of the cup, the stock closed at around $43. A few months later the price kept dropping until it reached the bottom of the cup, at $25. Volume should be declining. From the tip of the cup until the trough, there could be a difference of as much as 33 percent. When you only see half of a cup formed, it's not the time to buy yet because you don't know where the stock is headed. What if no pattern emerges after all?

Look at the right half of the cup. From the bottom, the stock price slowly rises over the next few months to complete the cup's rounded U-shape. Why does the stock recover? When it hit $25, investors who smell a bargain jump in. As more people buy the stock, its price rises. For AGRPA, the stock ascends to $52. Forming the cup could take as long as *three to six months*.

Go to the handle. After the stock hits $49, it drops to $46. What's going on? The people who bought in at the left tip of the cup—$43—got nervous when the stock dropped to $25. But as the stock recovered to $49, they started selling. They're not going through the stress of seeing their investments drop like that again! As they unload their stocks, the price drops to $46. Remember Uncle Louie and the "overhead supply"? They are waiting to break even so they can get out.

That's why you still don't want to buy when the stock hits the right tip of the cup. Overhead supply is present. If you had bought at $49, you'll ride the stock down through the bottom of the handle—$46—at which point you might be forced to sell based on the selling rules we'll go over later. Don't jump in yet. Now look at the volume bars underneath. They're getting smaller, meaning buying and selling are drying up. Overhead supply is disappearing. This is a good sign.

A few rules for the handle:

1. It should take more than one or two weeks to form. Healthy handles are five to seven weeks long.

2. The handle should point down (⌒⌒) not up (⌣).

3. The handle should fall in the *upper half* of the cup

When the stock rises to form the second half of the *handle*, it hits $48 and then—*boom!*—it jumps to $58 as the volume takes off too. The stock is now free from overhead supply; suddenly unrestricted, it surges.

It's time to switch your weekly chart for a *daily*. If you don't have access to daily charts through the Internet, check that newspaper *every day* now and make a mental note of the price and the volume change. We've seen the pattern emerge; now we're waiting for a buy signal. Remember, what we want is for the *closing price to rise by more than 1 percent from the previous day and volume to double its average volume for the last thirty days*. This is the *pivot*, or *buy point*.

If you see volume rise but not the price, sit tight. The stock could very well be headed the wrong way!

For Associated Group, the buy point is $48.48. How do we know?

Here's how to figure out 1 percent of a stock price:

Step 1: Take the current price and divide by one hundred (move the decimal point two places to the left).

Step 2: Add the figure from Step 1 to the current price.

In our example, the current price was $48 and 1 percent of it would be $0.48. Add the two together and you get $48.48.

Take a look at the closing price for the day before—$48. The jump from $48 to $58 was more than 1 percent. The stock has to beat $48.48 for the 1 percent rule to be fulfilled. Did Associated Group's price rise by more than 1 percent? You bet.

To see if volume rose by 100 percent (i.e., doubled) or more, simply multiply its average volume by two. Compare today's volume to this figure. The current volume has to be greater. For Associated Group, the average thirty-day volume is 165,000 shares. The company meets our volume standards as well. Its current volume of 1,086,700 shares certainly beats 165,000 shares.

Warning: Try to buy the stock as close to the pivot point as you possibly can. If you buy it too far off this price, you may be caught in a downtrend.

Let's review. When you see a cup-and-handle pattern, wait for the full design to form before jumping in. The cup could take three to six months to complete and the handle should be at least five to seven weeks long. Sometimes the cup part of the graph is flatter, making it look more like a bowl. Technical analysts call this pattern a *saucer with a handle*, but it is nothing more than the same dog wearing a different collar. Make sure the handle points down and it forms in the upper half of the cup. Switch to the daily stock chart when the handle is six weeks old so you are ready to jump on board as soon as you get the signal. Wait for a 1 percent or more increase in price *and* a 100 percent or greater rise in volume from the thirty-day average.

When your stock meets all these rules, drop what you're doing, take a sledgehammer to the piggy bank, and call your broker!

This is what happened after that buy signal from AGRPA:

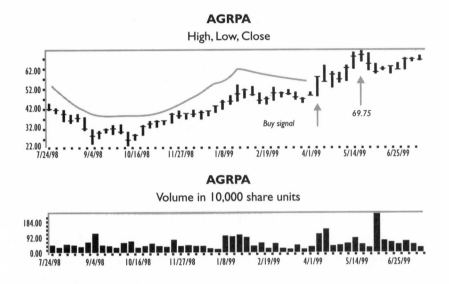

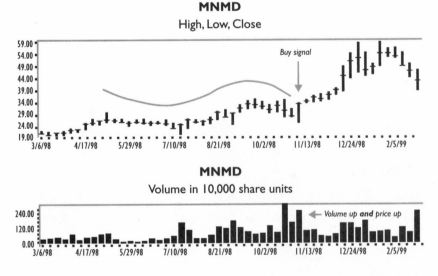

Associated Group climbed to $69.75 before it reversed its trend, a price increase of almost 44 percent over six weeks!

To help you get more attuned to the cup-with-a-handle pattern, here are more examples:

Source: AOL Historical Quotes

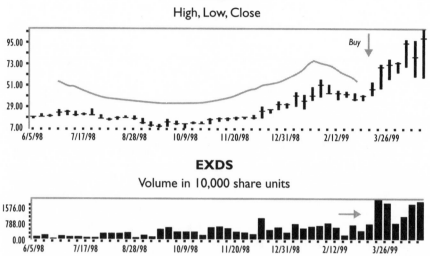

EXDS
High, Low, Close

EXDS
Volume in 10,000 share units

Double Bottom

It looks like a "W," two "V's" or a roller coaster. However you look at it, the technical term is a *double bottom*. The key to this pattern is that the second "V" is deeper than the first. As the stock price comes out of the second dip, it must pass the tops of the two "V's," or previous highs. Look for an increase in volume of at least 100 percent and a price rise of 1 percent or more from the day before. *That's when you buy.*

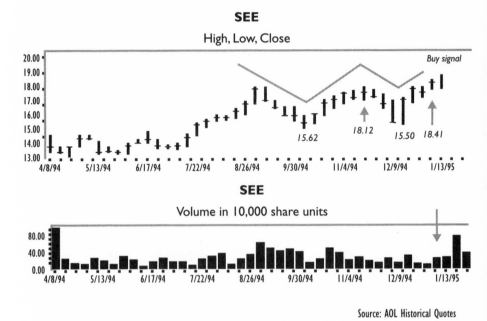

For example, look at the chart for Sealed Air Corp. (SEE), a containers and packaging company in Saddle Brook, New Jersey. You can see the two "V's," right? The bottom of the first "V" dropped to a close of $15.62. The second "V" declines to a low of $15.50. The second "V" plunged just below the first one, a healthy sign for a double-bottom pattern. Now look at the right tip of the second "V." Is it higher than the tops of the two "V's"? It sure is. Now wait for the pattern to meet our price and volume rules. On January 6, 1995, the price rose to $18.41 from a close of $17.74 the day before, with a higher-than-average volume. The buy point is right where it passes the right top of the first "V," in this case $18.12.

A double-bottom pattern can really put your stomach to the test. Just when you feel all is lost during the drop of the first "V," it turns around with a pickup in volume to give you hope. You may think the tide has reversed and you are now riding an uptrend, only to be disappointed once more when it tests your nerves by taking a second dive, this time past the first dip. How can you trust it now? Well, trust history. This pattern is one of the healthiest around. We just need to be disciplined enough to pay attention and wait until the right time to jump in. The right time is when the uptrend of the second bottom passes the previous high of the first "V" and continues to rise. Again, volume must confirm that we have made the right call—it has to reach double its thirty-day average trading volume.

Here are more examples of double bottoms:

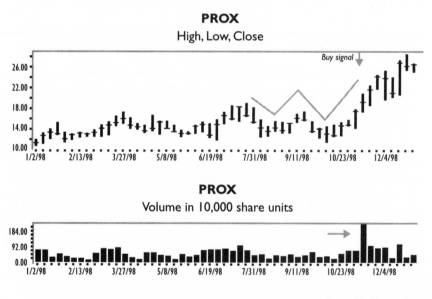

PROX
High, Low, Close

PROX
Volume in 10,000 share units

Source: AOL Historical Quotes

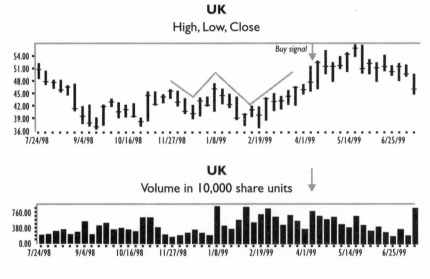

Source: AOL Historical Quotes

Wouldn't it be great if every stock chart we looked at formed one of the patterns we have discussed? That is not the case, however. Frequently, many stocks will be flying "wide and loose," not really doing anything in particular but going all over the place on that chart. Stay away from them. As you become familiar with the shapes of stock patterns, you will start to identify others that are perhaps not as significant as the ones we have mentioned, but helpful nonetheless. Meanwhile, use the trend lines and patterns we've learned as your guide.

Practice Session

Let's combine fundamental and technical analysis to determine whether a stock tip, JAKKS Pacific Inc., is a good buy.

First, go to www.marketguide.com to get the company profile. This is what you will find:

JAKKS Pacific, Inc. is engaged in the development, manufacture and marketing of toys and children's electronics products, some of which are based on character and product licenses.

Looking at the various reports on the company, we find that JAKKS has a *B*eta of 0.49. It is less than 1, thus it is less volatile than the market. The industry's beta is 1.02 and the sector has 0.94. The "B" on "BE A PROFIT" gets a check mark.

Next, we will analyze the earnings reports.

EARNINGS PER SHARE

Quarters	1996	1997	1998
MAR	0.010	0.050	0.080
JUNE	0.060	0.100	0.140
SEP	0.150	0.290	0.450
DEC	0.080	0.110	
Totals	**0.300**	**0.550**	

Note: Units in U.S. Dollars

Starting with the latest quarterly earnings-per-share figure, we see that JAKKS reported an EPS of forty-five cents in the September quarter. Comparing it with the same quarter a year ago—which had an EPS of twenty-nine cents—we calculate that JAKKS's earnings grew by 55 percent. Going back two previous quarters, we discover that the company's earnings grew by 40 percent. In terms of annual EPS, JAKKS looks good as well: Earnings rose 86 percent and 68 percent in the last three years.

E for *E*arnings gets a check.

What about *A*tmosphere? Looking at the charts for the Dow, the S&P 500, and the NASDAQ, we see the market heading upward. It's a good time to buy, so we check off "A."

The next letter we need to consider is "P" for the P/E ratio. JAKKS has a P/E of 25.89, lower than its industry's 40.74 and the S&P 500's 35.90. Right now the company is a good value compared with its industry. "P" gets a check as well.

How well is management handling investors' money? For JAKKS, the return on equity is 21.63, well above our 15 minimum standard. "R" gets a mark.

As for being an outstanding price performer, we will need to get a glimpse of the company's price-performance ranking. For the past fifty-two weeks, JAKKS came in at 93. Put a check on "O."

We come to the "F" in "BE A PROFIT," which is the float. JAKKS's float is 5.5 million shares. It meets our requirements.

Thus far, the company is looking good. As for institutional ownership, we find that 37.46 percent of outstanding shares are held by the heavy hitters. They also had a net purchase of sixty-thousand shares in the last quarter. The big spenders have noticed our company but there is still room for more of them. Check "I."

Finally, we get to "T" for top dollar. The company's fifty-two week high was 13 7/16 on July 28, 1998. At the time when we looked up JAKKS, the stock sold for $9.93. It's not the time to buy. The stock has to hit within 10 percent of its fifty-two-week high—or $12.09 and higher—for us to consider purchasing it.

Curious to see what the stock is doing now, we access the stock chart of JAKKS. We want to find some patterns emerge. Here is the one-year weekly chart for the company:

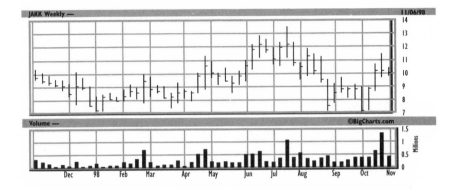

JAKKS Pacific took a deep plunge from July to October, mirroring the market's weakness. But look, at the end of October, we see two tall volume towers—trading has increased substantially and the stock's price rose. A new trend has begun. We should wait until the stock price reaches our buy point of $12.09. When it does, we're buying! Meanwhile, we watch.

It took JAKKS until January 7, 1999, to hit the buy price.

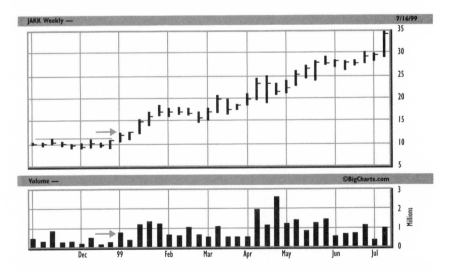

Notice that the stock was in a flat base pattern until it broke out and started an uptrend. By the end of June 1999, JAKKS Pacific was selling for $29 a share, a move of over 100 percent in just six months! Doesn't it pay to do your homework? Not every stock you find will perform as well as JAKKS, but with hard work and discipline, you will increase your chances of spotting these tremendous movers. Fellow wild women, we're going hunting!

CHAPTER SIX

Psychology and the Market

Remember a time when Beanie Babies were everywhere? Stores at the mall sold them. The neighborhood gift shops carried them. Magazines talked about the little critters. You could even buy them on the Internet. At first, you adored the squishy little animals. But you soon tired of them because they'd become so common. Every child including yours seemed to own at least one, if not dozens.

That's when you knew the Beanie Babies trend was waning. By the time all the stores had enough in stock, kids were off to the next thing. You cannot blame the retailers for being late. They have to wait for the manufacturer to ship them the toys. By the time the goods arrive, it's invariably too late. As a consumer, you can tell if a fad's fading—it happens when every store is selling it.

There is a lesson here for investors. When everyone is convinced that the market is invincible, that's when the end is near. Conversely, when people think the market is never going to improve, that is when it picks up. In this chapter, we will go over actual and psychological signs of the market. After all, gauging the health of the market is important. No matter how good your stock is, the market environment can tip the balance toward success or failure. When the market feels bad—the trend is downward—75 percent of your stocks may drop even if they are fundamentally sound companies. If the market's general direction is up, well-chosen stocks have a better opportunity to excel.

Markets come in two cycles: a bull and bear. A *bull market* is an environment where stock prices stay on an uptrend. The market rises and falls every day, but over the longer term, the overall direction is up. On average, it lasts about two years but may continue longer. A *bear market* is just the opposite; stock prices are heading down continually. The worst bear market in recent history was during 1973 and 1974. Stocks, as measured by the S&P 500, lost half of their value. Inflation was also high, which compounded the loss in terms of purchasing power.

Most economists agree that we have entered a bear market if there is a 15 percent decline from an index high and it lasts at least three months. Thankfully, bear markets tend not to hang around too long: They average nine months.

Bull and bear markets, therefore, are periods of time when the market follows a trend—up or down. However, in the midst of these markets, it is quite common to experience sudden drops in price. These are *corrections* and *crashes*.

A market correction is said to occur when there is a sudden, sharp decline of ten to 15 percent that lasts from a few days to a few weeks. A correction took place in October of 1997, when the S&P 500 lost about 10 percent of its value in a period of one week. So what is a crash? Let's just say that if a correction means the market is having a bad day, in a crash, it is having a horrendous day. On October 19, 1987, the Dow Jones Industrial Average dropped 22.6 percent. Although this crash occurred in a day, a crash may take several days or weeks.

When you see a correction or crash, it does not necessarily mean that we're heading into a bear market—although it could.

When to Invest

When we talked about the bull's-eye in chapter 3, remember I told you that it was important to assess the market's mood before you invest? We want to buy stocks during a bull market, not a bear, that is why the market indices have to be ascending. But there is more we can learn from the market.

Like a stock's price and volume, a market's level and volume also are good signals of when to invest and when to sell.

The best time to get into stocks is when the market reaches a bottom and is poised to head up again. How will you determine the bottom? Let's revisit our old friend the trend line.

Trend lines can be applied to the market just as they have proven useful in stock charts. The same rules apply to the market as they do to your stocks. Draw a line, following the trend of a market index. When the index crosses the line on a high-volume day, be prepared for a change in direction.

Another clue to a pending market shift is the performance of your own portfolio of stocks. Why? The market is composed of stocks like the ones you own. Before you see a mass movement in the market, little changes will begin showing up among individual stocks. The first trembles of the market are felt along the front lines—your investments.

How is your portfolio doing? Are your stocks up today? Are

they staying about the trend lines you have drawn? If you have invested in small-to-medium-size companies, you may get early signals about the health of the market. Investors who start to get nervous about the market's health will sell their small- and mid-cap stocks first and large-caps last. Smaller companies tend to be less stable; therefore, they will be discarded first. These are the kinds of companies we have; remember, we picked stocks with floats of 50 million or fewer shares.

When a stock's uptrend is broken, check the volume. If the number of shares being traded is significantly greater than normal, better get ready to sell!

When you have cashed out most or all your stocks, don't be chagrined that the market indices are still hitting new highs. That's the way it usually happens! It feels uncomfortable, even painful, to sell a stock while you are listening to Wall Street pundits talk about the Dow hitting record highs. However, bear in mind that market tops are missed by most people. You're getting out before the market turns nasty.

If you want a second and third opinion on market direction before cashing out, here are two more ways of reading the market.

Mechanical vs. Psychological

There are two kinds of tools to determine market direction: *mechanical*, which analyzes the charts of market indices, and the *psychological*, which will give us a whiff of crowd sentiment. In a toss-up between the two, mechanical is effective but psychological is just as good an indicator, if not better. This information is read-ily available in *Barron's*, a national financial publication.

Moving on . . . to Moving Averages

Among the most popular mechanical tools for assessing the condition of the market is a *moving average*.

A moving average is a line that you will often see on charts, whether on a market or stock chart.

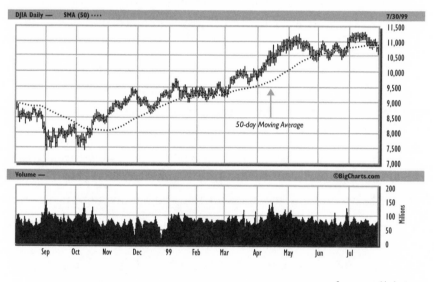

Source: www.bigcharts.com

Moving averages come in many forms, but we will discuss the most popularly used: the *simple or arithmetic moving average*. The moving average can range from as few as five days to two hundred days. One of the most common moving averages is the fifty-day moving average. To calculate a fifty-day moving average, you would add up the closing prices (of a market index or stock) of the last fifty days and divide by fifty. This number is plotted on a graph. Each day, a new closing price is added to the list of fifty and the first number on the list is dropped. Once again, these fifty numbers are added and the total is divided by fifty. This new figure is plotted next to yesterday's average and so on. Eventually, all the dots connect to form a line. You don't have to calculate the average yourself; many publications and Web sites already draw them for you.

Some market technicians believe that more weight should be given to recent prices. As such, they would rather use the *exponential moving average* because it does just that. However, for our purposes, when we refer to a moving average, we are talking about the simple average.

The major advantage of a moving average is its ability to smooth out the daily fluctuations of the market index. Think about it: The line is composed of *average* prices. Therefore, it won't show the actual, day-to-day, wild swings in the market.

However, the shorter the time period for a moving average, the closer it will reflect the actual daily graph itself. A two-hundred-day moving average will tell you the average price over two hundred days and will appear as a flatter line, gently sloping in the general trend of your index. In contrast, a fifty-day average, since it is composed of more recent prices, will more closely reflect the index. Look at the following chart for the Dow. The top curve shows the fifty-day moving average, the bottom, two-hundred-day:

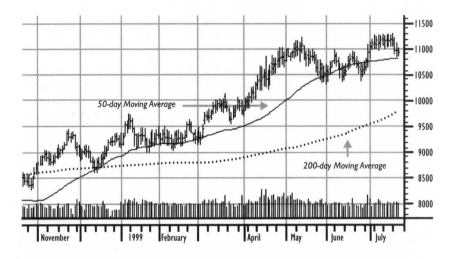

Notice that the Dow was decisively above the fifty-day line from April until the beginning of May. But in June, it started heading down and proceeded to make a series of zigzag bounces just below the fifty-day moving average. Finally, at the beginning of July, it rose past the moving average and the eleven-thousand mark and tried to go up higher, only to come back down again.

The fifty-day moving average will react faster to changes than the two-hundred-day; it parallels the actual Dow movement more closely.

I'm not saying that a short moving average is better. You don't want it too short. The purpose of a moving average is to look at the general trend, not react based on daily fluctuations. For our purposes, we will focus on the fifty-day average.

Let's go back to the chart. In June and July, when the Dow crisscrossed the fifty-day average, we should stay put and not buy stocks at the moment. The Dow is too close to the moving average. History has shown that when an index crosses a moving average, the market direction could change. That's why *you should wait until the Dow (or any index) is clearly above the fifty-day moving*

average because then you will be more confident of market direction.
Remember, don't make a move until you know.

What if the Dow, S&P 500, and NASDAQ do not agree on market direction? Follow the S&P 500. The other indices will follow.

Does Your Index Have "Bad Breadth"?

Is your index a stinker? We want an index that enjoys good breadth, not bad breadth. But how do we get a whiff?

First, we must understand the *advance/decline line*.

Each day, the bulls (buyers) and bears (sellers) get into a fight. Whoever wins will determine whether the market is going to be up or down for the day. When bulls win, the market rises because buyers outnumber sellers. When bears win, the market tumbles because sellers are holding court.

There is a quick way to measure this fight: with the advance/decline line. The line tells us whether there are more buyers or sellers on a given trading day. It is calculated by taking the number of New York Stock Exchange stocks that increase in price and subtracting the number of declining stocks. The result is added to a running tally. Stocks that close unchanged are not used. The bigger the difference between the number of rising and declining stocks, the more certain you can be of a definite trend.

For instance, if there are twice as many advancing stocks as decliners—it's a two-to-one ratio—that is a healthy market, since for every one stock dropping in price two are gaining. The market is said to have good breadth. But if it's three to two, meaning for every three stocks that have risen two went down, the market isn't as strong. Its breadth is smaller.

The opposite is true as well. When downs outnumber ups, a weak market is upon us because more stocks are being sold than bought. If the number of stocks weakening grows, the trend toward a down market is stronger. Hold your nose; this is bad breadth.

Obviously, we want the market to have good breadth. Check market charts for a rising a/d line that shows strong breadth. The a/d line should head in the same direction as an index. Be careful when new highs in the Dow and the S&P 500 are not confirmed by a rising a/d line. Both should be parallel. The a/d line should not be weakening or dropping off while the index surges forward. If it does, this tells us that while the Dow's thirty stocks or the S&P's five hundred companies are advancing, the rest of the stocks do not share their success. It's a sign of weakness. Eventually, the decline will catch up to the Dow and the S&P and drag them down.

In August 1987, two months before the one-day drop of 508 points in the Dow, the a/d line lagged behind as the Dow rallied to 2746. Here is what the Dow's daily chart looked like from September 1987 to November 1987. See the gap between the Dow and the a/d line slowly widening from late August until mid October?

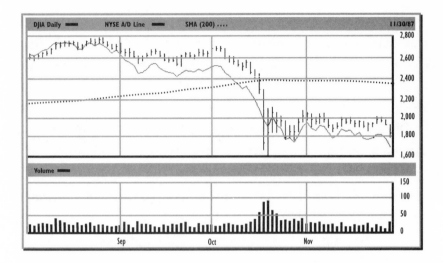

A Final Note: The a/d line reliably spots the end of a bull market (also called a market top). However, it is less able to pinpoint the start of a bull market, which is when the market reaches a bottom and begins to move up again.

Don't Follow the Leaders (or the Rank and File)

Let's explore the market's psychological indicators. The market is psychological? Sure! Who makes up the market? Investors. Won't you cheer when the market is strong and fret when it's not? Don't people sometimes buy stocks on a whim and sell when they are in a panic? Don't good rumors and nasty gossip prompt some people to invest or sell out? Of course. The market can be quite emotional.

With psychological indicators, we will get into the minds of the masses. By having a good idea of what they are thinking, we can use this information to know where the market is headed.

First, let me tell you a secret: Most Wall Street experts and investors cannot determine market direction. Yes, prevailing wisdom is mostly wrong; it doesn't matter how many letters they have after their names. Humbling, isn't it? According to Gerald M. Loeb in *The Battle for Investment Survival*, market forecasters are only right one-third of the time. Two-thirds of the time, they are dead wrong. That's a failing grade!

Are we saying that regular folks like Uncle Louie are right? No. The masses are off track too. They don't get it either; *most people cannot determine market direction*. When they think the good times will go on forever, a bear market is coming. When they are convinced the sun will never shine on the market again, that's when it will start improving. What can I say? It's the truth.

Financier and philanthropist John Marks Templeton hit the bull's-eye when he said, "Bull markets are born on pessimism, grow on skepticism, mature on optimism and die on euphoria." Therefore, our task is to find out what most people are thinking, then we act on the opposite of what they believe. For example, when everybody and their grandmother are putting the kids' college money into the market because it seems to rise forever—beware. Since the masses are wrong and they often react late in the game, when you see such strong and widespread optimism, start selling because a downturn is coming.

I'm not saying that you should snoop around your neighbors' house to know what people think about the market. Several psychological indicators published in *Barron's* give you a good idea of what investors think.

The Art of Reading Minds

Let's look at the following four indicators.

Bullish/Bearish Sentiment

In 1963, Investors Intelligence launched a survey of investment newsletters with the expectation that experts would correctly pick out market tops and bottoms. But to everyone's surprise, it turned out to be just the opposite. The survey discovered that investment advisory firms, taken as a group, are wrong most of the time because they follow the current trend. A contrary theory emerged: When most investment advisors are bullish (optimistic that the market will go up) and few are bearish (pessimistic and therefore predicting a drop in the market), the stock market is close to topping out and a drop is coming. When many advisors are bearish and only a small group is bullish, the market is near a bottom and poised to rise. But how much is "most" and "few"?

Good, bullish times are ahead if *less than 40 percent* of investment advisors are bullish and *more than 30 percent* are bearish. Watch for a market fall when bullishness is *greater than 50 percent* and bears are *fewer than 20 percent*. For example, if 35 percent of advisors are bulls and 55 percent are bears, a bull market is coming. Of course, don't just look at one set of numbers. Watch for repeating patterns before you conclude it's a trend. Account for degrees of market healthiness too. If bears stand at 35.2 percent and bulls at 47.6 percent, how do you read it? This is a healthy market since the two numbers are closer to the signs for a bull than a bear.

Short Selling by Odd-lotters

In the stock market, bulls buy a stock hoping it will appreciate. Bears think stock prices will head down, leading them to sell a stock outright or sell it *short*. In a short sale, an investor borrows stock from a broker and sells it to someone else in the market. Then she waits, hoping the stock will fall. When it does, she buys the stock at a lower price and pays the broker what she owes. The short seller keeps the profit.

Stocks usually are bought or sold in groups of one hundred shares. It's called a *round lot*. But investors who can't afford to buy a round lot may purchase as few as one, five, ten, or any number of shares under one hundred. This is called an *odd lot*, and they, the *odd-lotters*.

Odd-lotters are viewed as the least sophisticated of investors. In this group, those who short-sell are even more naive. They hear about a trend, and when they finally act, it's too late. You could call them the Rodney Dangerfields of the investment world: They get no respect. Not surprisingly, the trades of odd-lot short sellers are one of the best gauges of crowd psychology. The more odd-lotters short-sell, believing the market is going down, the better the odds that it's going to be a bull. *They are just plain wrong.*

You can find a snapshot of odd-lotter's activities in *Investor's Business Daily*. A 4.0 or higher figure here is a positive sign. It says odd-lotters are pessimistic, therefore, the market may be poised for an upturn.

Watching the Specialist

Just as the behavior of naive investors gives us clues about the market, so do the actions of the sophisticated. Among them are the New York Stock Exchange specialists. Remember them from chapter 2? They are the people on the exchange floor who bridge gaps between trades to make sure each buyer will find a seller and vice versa. Each specialist deals in several stocks. They also trade using their own accounts to provide market depth and price continuity in their speciality stock. Unlike odd-lotters, specialists are quite savvy when they short-sell. Follow their lead: If they are short-selling more, it means they're bearish. If less, they are bullish.

The ratio of total public short sales versus specialist short sales is a widely followed indicator. If it's above 0.6, meaning fewer short sales among specialists, the market is likely to go higher. When the ratio is 0.35 or below, it's bearish.

Mutual Fund Share Purchases vs. Redemptions

It's time to reunite with our old friends, the institutional investors. Because they have a big influence on the market, we want to observe their behavior. Let's go visit with one in particular, the mutual fund. If the fund is receiving a lot of money from investors, the manager has more money to invest in the stock market. When a mutual fund buys, it causes prices to rise. The opposite, of course, is when investors withdraw money from their mutual funds. In a *redemption*, fund managers have to sell stock for cash in order to meet the withdrawal requests. When these institutions sell stock, prices drop.

Of course, investors put money into, and withdraw money from, mutual funds all the time. But one has to look at the overall result: If investments into funds are larger than redemptions, there is more money to buy shares in the market. If redemptions outflank investments, the market could weaken.

CHAPTER SEVEN

Knowing When to Let Go

You call her old Betsy and you love her to death. Indeed, she is slowly dying but you will not let go. You will not pull the plug. No matter how badly your beloved twenty-year-old Ford Country Squire station wagon behaves—*chug, chug, sputter, sputter, hiss, hiss*—you will not ditch her. Never. How could you? It's a family album on wheels. The crayon marks on the backseat? Jimmy was two when he did that. The stain on the floor of the front seat? Katie spilled grape juice there on the way to the park one day. The dent on the side? Matt's first try at driving. The kids even had a fond name for her—the B-1 Bomber. Tears fill up your eyes at the memories. How could you possibly part with your Betsy?

It's time to let her go. She needs a new carburetor and transmission. Betsy goes to the shop once a month now, straining your budget to the limit. Wouldn't it be better to get another car than waste more money on repairs when you know the end is near? There comes a time when change is necessary and good.

In investing, we should also know when to call it quits. Even after much research, we can still make mistakes. That's life. However, by sticking to a set of selling rules, you will know when to pull the plug so you will cut your losses quickly to prevent a large-scale disaster.

It's like dating. No one starts dating someone anticipating they will break up, but sometimes things just don't work out. But isn't it better to end the relationship early rather than marrying, having kids, and ending up in a messy divorce later? So even when you are losing money on a stock, once you see a sell signal, dump it. It's okay. True success in investing does not mean making money with every investment. *It's when profits well outweigh losses.*

You are going to get your share of duds. One of the biggest mistakes investors make is to hold losers in hopes of a comeback. Women especially tend to nurture stocks. We think all a losing stock needs is tender loving care and it will reward us by coming back to life. "I bought the stock at $25 and it's now $15 a share," you say. "Surely, it can't go lower." Guess again. It can drop to zero. Even major corporations don't always come back from the dead. Remember PanAm? That stock's surely grounded.

In previous chapters, we learned how to buy stocks. Now we will turn our attention to an often ignored but equally important investment strategy: when to sell. Have the courage to admit that you have made a mistake, cut your losses, and get on with life. It's like missing an off-ramp on the highway. Get off at the next exit. You will never reach your destination if you keep heading the wrong way.

The following rules are exit signs for an investor. If a stock meets one or more of them, you know what to do—give it the old heave-ho and don't look back!

Rule No. 1: A stock drops by 10 percent from the purchase price

You finally bought the stock you have tracked for months. At last, both fundamental and technical analyses agree it's a buy. Feeling a little nervous and excited at the same time—you are playing with the big boys of Wall Street now—you take the plunge. With bated breath, you hope for success. But instead of appreciating, the stock keeps drifting down. It drops a quarter point one day, an eighth the next. What should you do—hold or sell? Since you did your due diligence, it should have taken off right away. But the stock's declining; you've made a mistake.

Sell when the price drops by 10 percent from the buy point. For example, if the stock cost you $100 a share, sell at $90. You don't need to be right every time to make money in the market. As long as you are willing to cut your losses early, your chances of making a profit in the long run will improve.

Rule No. 2: You've made a profit

Congratulations! You correctly identified the buy point and courageously bought the stock. As a reward, it started rising just as you had hoped. Soon, you have gotten a nice profit. You want the good times to last forever. As a realistic investor, you also know that success might be short-lived. It's time to think about protecting your gains.

Historically, after successful stocks move up from their buy point, they start to decline or consolidate. Remember our trends? Draw your trend lines and be on the lookout for a trend reversal. You don't want to make a gain and then lose it.

I have found that most people have more trouble selling a winning stock than a losing one. It makes me sad to think of all the investors I've met who do not use selling rules. They see their stocks hit new highs and then slide bit by bit until there is no profit left. That's why we need to have a plan in place whether our stock sinks or soars.

Once you buy a stock and it keeps moving up, set your sell points consistently higher. For example, if you paid $30 a share, your initial sell point to protect your investment is $27. If your stock goes up to $33, your new sell point will be 10 percent below this high—$30. You want to defend your profits, not just your initial investment. If the stock moves up more to $35, your selling point is $31.50. Keep moving the sell point up each time the stock rises.

You are still allowing it some room to correct, but not enough to take back the profit it has given to you. If your stock starts losing steam and breaks through that 10 percent from-the-top barrier, it may be time to kiss it good night and move on.

Accountants may warn you about the capital gains taxes you will have to pay by selling your holdings. My philosophy has always been this: If paying capital gains is the worst thing I have to face as an investor, then I welcome it! It's better to protect your profits, even if you have to pay Uncle Sam, rather than take a loss. I do not base my stock choices on tax rules; I base them solely on the merits of the stocks I buy.

Rule No. 3: New highs on lower volume

Right out of the gate, your stock keeps climbing. It's exhilarating to watch it rise like a balloon in the sky. Every time you check on the stock, it makes you giddy to see how much profit you are making. But watch for warning signs. *When the stock continues to climb but volume is dropping, prepare to sell.* It's a sign of weakening demand for the stock.

Higher price together with slowing demand means there is still some buying going on, but not much. Most people—especially the institutional investors—are not buying anymore. Without backup from institutions, sellers will soon overpower the buyers and drive down the price. It's time to sell.

Another warning sign is when a stock starts the trading day at a low price and persists in this manner for several days. Once it starts the day down in the dumps, it does not recover or rally. Volume is light. Sell it. In a way, doesn't this remind you of the last embers of a dying relationship? You know the signs: He is not excited to be with you anymore. He would rather hang out with his friends. Suddenly you are the nag. Cut him loose. Move on.

Rule No. 4: Moving fast and going nowhere

For this, you will need to watch the stock's *intraday movements*—movement within a day. Observe the full swing of its price—how high it reached and how low it dropped—and record it. Do this for at least a week. For example, a stock may hit a high of 102⅜ and a low of 95¹⁄₁₆ on Monday. On Tuesday, it goes up to 101¾ and drops as far as 93³⁄₁₆. The following day, it climbs to a peak of 100⁵⁄₁₆ and declines to a valley of 92. A newspaper's stock tables will have this information.

Now what? Once you know how the price swings, see where the stock closes for each of the trading days. When it ends the day at or near the day's low point, watch out. The stock is weak. It tried to end the day near the high, but failed because it could not muster enough buyers. Get ready to sell.

Rule No. 5: Quarterly earnings slow down or decrease

You have picked a good stock and it has done well for you. The company's fundamental foundations are sound: earnings have been healthy, increasing at a fast clip. That's why you are not concerned at all about tomorrow's earnings report. It's got a good track record, right? Profits should be robust, as always.

Then the unthinkable happens. To your and Wall Street's surprise, the company announces much slower growth in quarterly earnings than previous periods. Accustomed to a 30 percent or higher growth rate, your beloved company said earnings rose by only 15 percent this time. Do not panic. It's just one time. Every company, even the best ones, has a slower quarter now and again. However, if profits decelerate or decline in the next quarter, phone your broker and place a sell order. We want a company that's getting stronger, not weaker. Remember, the biggest booster of a company's stock price is its earnings.

Rule No. 6: Stops being an outstanding performer

Remember the "O" in BE A PROFIT? We insisted that a stock's rank in the industry be at least 80, meaning its price has gone up higher than 80 percent of its peers. It's a strong stock because investors are buying it in droves. So what is a weakening stock? *If its ranking falls below 70, demand for the stock has fallen and it might be a good time to sell.*

CHAPTER EIGHT

Mutual Funds—How to Let Others Work for You

Stepping into the busy street outside her apartment building, Karen flagged down a taxicab with practiced ease. "Four forty-five Madison Avenue, please," she tells the driver as he pulls over. In forty-five minutes, she will be pitching an advertising campaign to executives of Baby's Bounty Corp. The company is launching a new line of all-natural baby food and she's heading the team assigned to the account. Settling into the cab's slightly battered backseat, she mentally goes over her presentation. She usually drives to work, but today she didn't feel like battling rush hour traffic. She'll let someone else drive and get to the meeting relaxed. It's too important a presentation to botch.

Similarly when you invest in a mutual fund, you are letting someone else do the driving. Perhaps you don't have time to properly research and track a stock or you are not yet confident of your own abilities. Maybe you don't want the hassle. Whatever the reason, it makes sense to let other people invest your money as long as they have an excellent track record. In this chapter, I will teach you how to pick a good mutual fund. Then sit back, relax, and let the driver handle it!

How a Mutual Fund Works

During one of my seminars, a young woman sitting in the back raised her hand and said: "I know I should know this because I have one, but what's a mutual fund?"

Let's start our lesson by understanding how a mutual fund works. If you recall from Chapter 1, a mutual fund is a "basket" of money gathered from investors like you and me. The pool of money is handled by a mutual fund manager, who will invest the funds for us for a fee. The manager is employed by a mutual fund company—a business that oversees a group of funds.

Mutual funds have been around since the 1920s but their popularity has soared in the past fifteen years. Today more than 40 million people own a mutual fund; that's one out of every three households. Yet, these investments are widely misunderstood.

One of the most common misconceptions is that funds, especially if they are bought from a bank, are federally insured. Unlike your bank savings or checking account, they are not. Your investments *will* rise and fall, and this is a risk you have to take. However, unlike the banking and savings-and-loan industries, there has yet to be a mutual-fund-company collapse.

Mutual funds offer three ways to make a profit: *dividends*, *capital gains distributions*, and *redemptions*.

When the fund manager invests the money in the fund, he may choose to buy many things—stocks, bonds, and other securities. Some of these investments may pay dividends. Remember?

A *dividend* is part of the company's profit that it gives back to shareholders. When a mutual fund buys stock in a company that pays dividends, the fund receives them. In turn, the dividends are passed on to investors in the mutual fund. You may choose to receive the dividends in cash, or reinvest them into the fund.

When the fund manager decides to sell some of the stocks, bonds, or other securities, he or she may make a profit on them. These profits are distributed to investors of the fund as capital gains distributions. Again, you may choose to take cash for it, or reinvest the money back into the fund. If the manager loses money on an investment, the loss is passed along to you as well.

Another way to make money is to cash out your investment from the fund. After you have invested your money for a time and see a profit, you may decided to withdraw your funds. This is called a *redemption*.

Open and Closed

There are two species of funds: *open end* and *closed end*. An *open-end fund* is one that accepts money from new investors all the time. It is always open to the public. In rare instances, an open-end fund may close itself temporarily to new investors if it cannot handle all the money coming in. For instance, the Janus Twenty Fund closed its doors to new investors in mid-1999 after an excellent performance in 1998 brought in a flood of new money.

A *closed-end fund* acts more like a stock than a traditional mutual fund. First of all, you cannot put money into the fund because it is a publicly traded investment company. Just like a corporation, a closed-end fund raises money by offering stock to the public and its stock price is quoted daily. Investors make money by buying and selling its stock on an exchange, much like you would IBM. In an open-end fund, investors can put money in and take money out of the fund. In a closed-end fund, investors buy and sell its stock to other investors in the market.

For our purposes, we will only talk about open-end funds.

Fund Families: Normal or Dysfunctional?

When the same company handles a group of mutual funds, these funds are called a mutual fund family. Vanguard, T. Rowe Price, and Fidelity are examples of fund families. Under the umbrella of their name, each of these companies has many mutual funds from which you could choose, ranging from highly conservative to extremely aggressive.

Here is a typical mutual fund family tree:

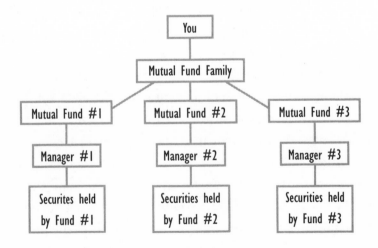

To protect the public, every mutual fund family has to follow rules set forth by the Securities and Exchange Commission. These rules apply to the funds themselves. They limit how much a fund can invest in a specific company or industry, or perhaps a type of security. The government wants to prevent fund managers from risking a good portion of the fund's money in one or two places. By placing their eggs in a few baskets, the managers will substantially increase the fund's risks. Mutual funds are mandated by law to invest in many securities to minimize risk. When one investment drops, chances are another security is making money and the two balance each other out. There's a small likelihood that all the investments will drop at once.

This is why novice investors start with mutual funds. They are less volatile than individual stocks, yet a stock mutual fund still provides exposure to the market. Funds also ease a new investor's transition into investing because she is getting help from the mutual fund manager. Granted, it's a mutual effort: She picks a good fund and the manager handles the money. However, the investor still has to monitor the fund from time to time to make sure it is performing.

Children of the Fund Families

Like the variety we find in our own families, fund families also have unique offspring. These children are all mutual funds, but they vary in personality. Some are aggressive, some are passive, and some are in between. How can you tell what kind of fund it is? By looking at its objective.

Common stock funds

As you can probably guess, these are funds that invest in common stocks. They are classified into four general categories, depending on how risky they can be and how much they give back in dividends.

- *Aggressive Growth.* When a fund describes itself as aggressive, it invests in smaller companies. An aggressive investment means there are more risks to be borne but there is also a greater chance of higher rewards. Growth indicates that the stocks being purchased are companies that don't distribute dividends. Instead, they pour profits back into the business to fuel growth. A fund makes money if these stocks appreciate in price. It doesn't count on dividends for profits. Therefore, an aggressive growth fund buys smaller companies poised for growth. There are about 155 aggressive growth funds. These include Fidelity New Millennium, Janus Olympus, and Putnam Voyager.

- *Growth.* A growth fund invests in large, established companies that may not pay dividends but shovel profits back into the company to boost growth. Microsoft is the most famous example of a growth company. Despite its size, the software maker is still registering double-digit earnings growth. It also doesn't pay dividends, to investors' dismay. There are about two thousand growth funds, including such names as Janus Twenty, Gabelli Growth, and Vanguard Primecap.

- *Growth and Income.* We've gone over the growth part. Income stocks are companies purchased for their dividends. Combining the two, this fund looks for blue-chip companies whose stock prices are expected to accelerate *and* they also pay dividends. Domini Social Equity, Pioneer, and AIM Blue Chip are among the more than eight hundred choices available in this category.

- *Sector.* Funds that invest in stocks of a single industry or sector are called sector funds. There are hundreds of sector funds available today. They offer investors a convenient and more diversified way to invest in a particular industry without having to choose only one company in particular. However, since the funds' focus is only in one industry, sector funds are known to have a higher volatility than general equity funds. Fidelity Select Computers is an example of a sector fund. If you see the name of a specific segment of the stock market like gold or utilities as part of your fund name, chances are you've invested in a sector fund.

Fixed Income Funds

These are funds that invest in bonds. Recall that bonds are IOUs. Bonds issued by companies are called corporate bonds. Those from the government are government or treasury bonds. Municipal bonds are those issued by state and local governments. Investors who prefer stability over a high return on their money tend to choose bond funds.

* *Government Bonds.* Since bonds are loans, investors who buy bonds are lending someone money in exchange for a return of the principal plus interest. Government bond funds invest in IOUs from federal, state, and local governments. Unlike stocks, the returns on government bond funds are much lower. There are three types of government bonds: U.S. Treasury bills, with maturities from ninety days to one year; U.S. Treasury notes, which are bans that mature from one to ten years; and U.S. Treasury bonds, which have maturities from ten to thirty years. Other government bonds include debt from agencies of the federal government such as the Government National Mortgage Association, also known as Ginnie Mae (GNMA). Funds in this group include American Century Target, Rushmore U.S. Government Bond, and Lexington GNMA Income.

* *Corporate Bonds.* These are IOUs from companies. Since they are not as stable as the U.S. government, they have to pay a higher interest to entice investors to lend them money. However, the interest paid on corporate bonds varies, depending on the stability of the company involved. A highly regarded and established company such as AT&T will pay a lower interest rate than a less stable company. Again, AT&T is seen as a safer investment while the smaller company will have to pay a higher interest to attract investors. A company's bonds are rated according to the financial health of the business. The highest ratings a corporate bond could get are AAA, AA, or A. Mutual funds that invest in high-quality corporate bonds include Dodge & Cox Income and Scudder Income.

* *High-Yield or Junk Bonds.* These funds buy bonds that are rated BB or below. Companies that issue these bonds are considered a higher risk because of problems with their operations. Before

Macy's was swallowed up by Federated Department Stores, its bonds got a junk rating due to a Chapter 11 bankruptcy. However, Macy's bond holders were amply rewarded as the retailer's business improved. Indeed, managers of this kind of fund bet on companies whose fortunes might improve. For risks taken, the interest payoff is high. T. Rowe Price High Income and Oppenheimer Champion Income mutual funds fall under this category of lower-quality bond funds.

* *Municipal (Tax-Exempt) Bond Funds.* "Muni" bond funds, as they are commonly called, invest in municipalities for projects such as building libraries and bridges. They provide the investor with an even greater tax advantage since they may be exempt from federal, state, and local taxes.

Funds with Stocks, Bonds, and Other Securities

Some mutual funds prefer to invest in a variety of securities. Since different securities react differently to economic factors, fund companies believe this is a good way to minimize volatility. However, it may come at a cost to an investor's return.

* *Balanced.* This type of fund invests between 60 and 70 percent of its money in stocks and the rest in bonds. It tries to balance the movements of stocks and bonds, which thrive under different economic conditions. An all-stock fund is diversified because it invests in at least twenty companies, as mandated by the SEC. The risks carried by the companies are minimized. However, stocks as a category still react the same way under certain economic conditions. By adding bonds, the fund diversifies

further by bringing in a new kind of security. Pax World and Janus Balanced belong to this group.

* *Foreign/International and Global.* Doesn't it seem that foreign, international, and global mean the same thing? In the world of mutual funds, foreign and international carry the same meaning, but they are distinct from global. A foreign or international fund invests only in securities outside the U.S. It is not allowed to buy a U.S. stock. On the other hand, a global fund can invest in both the U.S. and abroad. It even has the discretion of putting all its money in American companies or 100 percent in non-U.S. firms. Putnam International Growth is an example of an international fund. Citizens Global Equity fall under the global fund category.

* *Index.* In the past decade, these funds have enjoyed great popularity because they mimic market indices. They buy securities that are part of an index they wish to mirror. For example, the Vanguard Index 500 fund buys all the stocks in the Standard & Poor's 500. Whatever stock is in the S&P 500, you'll find it in Vanguard as well. Why? A mutual fund's performance is usually compared with the S&P 500. Since it is hard to beat the index—nine out of ten managers don't—Vanguard came up with an idea: If you can't beat it, join it! It created a fund that mirrors the S&P. Today, the Vanguard Index 500 is the second largest and one of the most successful funds in America.

A Word About Money Market Funds

A money market fund is a funny thing. It acts like a mutual fund and a checking account. Although money market funds are not guaranteed, they are considered a very stable investment which pays you dividends in a checking account environment. This fund invests in short-term debt of companies, treasury bills, and the like. A money market fund is a better alternative to bank certificates of deposit. It offers free check-writing privileges and your money is never tied up. However, you usually have to write large checks—the minimum is $250 to $500. Current returns range from about 4 percent to 6 percent on taxable money market funds. These yields fluctuate on a daily basis.

Money market funds are a great place to hold money that you will need access to fairly quickly. Perhaps you are saving for a down payment on a car, a vacation, or a special art piece. A money market fund is a good place to park your money.

Stocks vs. Bonds: Which Is Safer?

On the surface, bonds may seem a safer investment than stocks. After all, debt has to be repaid, right? With stocks, you can lose your entire investment. It's a convincing argument, but let me suggest to you that bonds can be risky too.

It all comes down to the secondary market.

Say what?

Let's imagine that you bought a bond for $10,000 from the Acme Co. It pays 7 percent interest and the bond's term is ten years. Providing Acme doesn't go under, you'll get 7 percent interest on your money every year. At the end of ten years, you will get the $10,000 back.

Meanwhile, life happens. You have a teenager at home and expenses are piling up. You need the $10,000 back. But your $10,000 is tied up. Heading for your broker, you plead with her: "I know I said ten years, but I need the money now!" The broker replies, "No problem. I'll get rid of that bond for you." She doesn't go to Acme, since it already received your $10,000. The deal is done. Instead, she taps the bond market—a swap meet where investors buy and sell bonds. This is the *secondary market.*

Think of it this way: If you changed your mind about a designer dress and the retailer refused to take it back, how do you get rid of it? Find another person to buy it. That's the same way you get rid of bonds. The company usually doesn't take it back, so you have to sell it to another investor.

Let's say the market is currently selling bonds like yours but with a 5 percent interest rate. Your bond, which pays 7 percent, is a better deal than what is available. So when your broker tries to sell it, she will probably get plenty of offers. Many people would want it. A savvy broker would say, "The price now is $11,000, not $10,000." The bond is selling at a premium.

What if interest rates are at 10 percent when your bond goes on sale? The broker won't get many responses. Any prospective buyer can get a squeaky-new $10,000 bond that will pay 10 percent, so why should she buy yours when it pays only 7 percent? Your broker will have to lower the bond's price to sell it. This is called *selling at a discount.*

Remember: Prices and rates move opposite to each other. When interest rates increase, the price of bonds drops. When rates decline, the price of bonds rises.

When you sell bonds, you are at the mercy of interest rates. The longer a bond's term, the more sensitive it is to rates.

Thus, bond funds can be just as risky as stocks. A manager who actively trades bonds instead of holding them to maturity faces the same price fluctuations as a stock fund manager.

How to Open an Account in a Mutual Fund

It starts with you and your money. Once you have chosen a fund, call the fund family for an application form and a prospectus. The prospectus is a report of the mutual fund's goals, performance and costs. It also tells you the minimum amount of money you need to invest—usually $1,000 to $2,500 to open the account. For individual retirement accounts (IRAs), which you can't withdraw from until after the age of fifty-nine and a half, the minimum initial investment is lower—usually $500. However, if you choose direct deposit, where the fund withdraws automatically from your bank account, you can start investing with as little as $50 a month or $12.50 a week. Direct deposit also has another advantage: It forces you to invest regularly and buy in at different fund prices. Thus, you will get in when the market's high and when it is low. This practice is called *dollar-cost averaging*. Because your costs average out, it prevents you from buying in high all the time.

When you invest in a fund, you are buying shares in it. Shares? "I thought only companies had shares," you say. Mutual funds do too. When a fund is first created, it gathers a pool of money from investors. How can it tell investors how much of the fund they own? How will it distribute gains and losses? The way they do it is with shares. The fund decides on a number of outstanding shares it will offer. After taking in investors' money and expenses are subtracted, the amount is divided by the number of shares to get a share price. If the fund collects $10 million after costs and it has 500,000 shares, each share will cost $20. If you send the mutual fund $1,000, you will own fifty shares.

This share price is called the *net asset value*. Every trading day, a mutual fund recalculates the NAV since money is flowing in and out of the fund all the time. The fund adds up investors' money, subtracts expenses, and divides by the number of shares to get the net asset value for the day. The NAV is listed in the stock tables under mutual funds or found on the Internet.

However, the NAV is not always the price at which investors can buy a share. Funds that charge a commission, or load, add their markup to the NAV. This is what investors pay.

How to Pick a Winning Fund

When choosing a mutual fund, you might be tempted to invest in the one your broker or someone else recommends. After all, they told you it had an 11 percent return in 1999. Not bad. It certainly beats bank CDs. What if I told you that you could have made almost 25 percent in a similar fund that carried less risk than the market? Your jaw would probably drop. The lesson here is to comparison-shop. How else would you know whether you have a good catch? Out of over 10,000 mutual funds, how is yours doing? Not sure? Let me teach you how to screen funds.

First, understand that a mutual fund is always compared with the S&P 500. It is every stock fund manager's goal to beat the Standard & Poor's 500 Index. Still, less than 10 percent of all funds succeed in doing so. Since the index is the benchmark to beat, why don't we check out the Vanguard Index 500 fund, which mimics the S&P? Let's head to the library for the Morningstar reports or crank up our computer to do some research.

Going to www.quote.com, we see mutual fund reports by Lipper and Morningstar, two highly respected authorities in the field.

Looking up Vanguard Index 500, here's what we get:

PERFORMANCE AS OF 07/26/99

I Week Performance	−4.20%	26 Week Performance	8.30%
I Year Performance	19.80%	Year to Date Performance	10.40%
3 Year Performance	30.50%	3 Year Total Return	122.40%
5 Year Performance	26.80%	5 Year Total Return	227.50%
10 Year Performance	17.50%	10 Year Total Return	402.90%
Performance Since Inception	15.70%	Total Return Since Inception	2710.30%
Quintile Rank—I year	I	Numeric Rank—I year	
Quintile Rank—3 years	I	Numeric Rank—3 years	
Quintile Rank—5 years	I	Numeric Rank—5 years	

Source: quote.com

Looking at our table, we see that the one-year return was 19.8 percent, the three-year averaged 30.50 percent for *each year*, and the five-year annual average was 26.8 percent. Getting excited? Don't buy it yet. Let's keep checking.

The figures at the bottom of the table, tell us the rank. If my fund is swimming in a sea of mutual funds, how is it competing? Is it a leader or a laggard? Vanguard Index 500's rank had been "1" consistently for the past five years. A "1" rating means its performance is in the top 20 percent of all funds with the same investment objective.

At this point skeptics may say that Vanguard did well in the last few years because we've had a strong bull market. That's a good point. A mutual fund may perform well in an up market but crumble in a downtrend. The following report tells us how the mutual fund fared in an up and down market:

RATINGS

Performance Quintile—Current	1	Universal Performance Quintile—Current	2
Performance Quintile—Up	1	Universal Performance Quintile—Up	3
Performance Quintile—Down	4	Universal Performance Quintile—Down	3

Source: quote.com

Let's read it from top to bottom, starting with the left side. In the top tier on the left, it says "Performance Quintile—Current." The rank is "1." When compared with all other funds with the same objective, this fund is currently in the top 20 percent. "Performance Quintile—Up," tells us how Vanguard Index 500 fared during the last upward trend in the market: also a "1." The last tier on the left tells us how the fund performed during the last downturn: a "4," meaning it landed in the bottom 40 percent of its kindred funds.

The right-hand side of the chart compares the fund with *all* other mutual funds, not just those with similar objectives.

Vanguard Index 500 is currently among the top 40 percent of

all funds, as you can see from "2" in the top tier on the right. Now we know that Vanguard is a leader in its category and lands in the top half when compared with all funds.

GENERAL

NAV	124.59	NAV Change	−0.85
Offer	124.59	Investment Category	Growth & Income
Total Net Assets ($millions)	92,643	as of	06/30/99
Yield	1.10%	as of	05/31/99
Volatility	4.78%	Beta	1.00

Source: quote.com

The objective of our fund, according to this table, is growth and income. The NAV price was $124.59. Since the offer price is also 124.59, I can see that this is a no-load fund. A difference in price between the two would be the load or markup. Offer is the price you would pay to buy the fund and NAV is the price you pay to sell it. In this case, they are equal. We'll go over this concept again when we talk about fees and charges.

The beta for the Vanguard Index 500 is "1," just like the S&P 500. Since this fund invests in the same five hundred stocks that make up the index, it would make sense that they share the same beta. Recall that beta measures risk. When a broker tells you that she can get you into a fund that earned 35 percent last year, don't jump in with joy. Ask her, "What's the beta?" It might have stellar returns, but if the beta is 3, can you sleep at night? The fund is three times as volatile as the S&P 500! If you know the S&P 500 made a nice 30 percent return in the same year and yet carries a beta of 1, shouldn't you get a higher return on your fund since it carries more risks? Again, shop around. A better fund for you might be either one that returns a hefty 28 percent with a beta of 0.87 or one that makes a 53 percent gain with a beta of 2.

I'll Buy It, But How Much Does It Cost?

Mutual funds invest your money for a fee. There are four places where they can "hide" this fee. These expenses can be *front-end loads, back-end loads, expense ratios* and *12b-1 fees*.

OPERATION

Fund Family	VANGUARD GROUP	Toll Free Phone	800-662-7447
Manager Name	George U. Sauter	Manager Tenure	1987
Max Sales Charge	0.00%	12b-1 Fee	0.00%
Redemption Fee	0.00%	Min Investment ($)	3000
Fiscal Year End	12/31/98	Expense Ratio	0.18%
Income Dividends ($)	1.33	Capital Gains Dividends ($)	0.76
Distrib Frequency	Quarterly		
Periodic Investment Plan?	Yes	Systematic Withdrawal Plan?	Yes

Source: quote.com

Front-end Load

This is probably the most publicized fee of a mutual fund. It's common to see fund advertisements claiming that they do not charge a front-end load. A load is a sales commission or charge. A front-end load is a sales commission investors pay every time they put money in the fund. The law allows the fee to be as high as 8.5 percent, but it rarely is this high due to competition. A quick way to spot a front-end load fund: when you see an "/A" after the fund's name. Looking at our chart, we see that Vanguard doesn't have a front-end load.

Frequently, a fund can call itself a no-load fund, meaning it does not charge a front-end load. Investors might think they're pretty smart to buy only these funds. Not necessarily. When I hear people say, "I only invest in no-load funds," and think they are getting in for free, I stifle an urge to laugh. Sure, there's no up-front charge. But the funds will get you somewhere else. They can inflate three other expenses to make up for the lack of a front load. Are they being sneaky? Maybe, but it's legal. However, investors can outsmart them by reading the fund's prospectus, which is sent along to you with your application form. You will find all the fees disclosed here.

Back-end Load

Funds may not charge you on the way in—like in front-end loads—but they may charge you on your way out. How? With the back-end load or *redemption fee*. Every time money leaves your account, you get hit with a charge. Thankfully, the back-end load gets smaller until it eventually disappears, usually in five years. A fund with this type of load, for example, may charge 5 percent in the first year, 4 percent the second year, and so on until the fee disappears altogether. If you want to withdraw money from your fund before the back-end load disappears, you will be charged according to the length of time you have been in it. This practice aims to discourage shareholders from withdrawing from their accounts early. A fund with a "/B" at the end of its name indicates a back-end load. Vanguard doesn't have a back-end load.

Expense Ratio

Mutual funds have expenses just like any other business. There is rent to pay, telephone charges, supplies, salaries, etc. These expenses are paid from the profits of the fund before they are distributed to you, the shareholder. The expense ratio is calculated by dividing the total amount of fees incurred by a fund by the average assets invested in the fund. Vanguard carries an expense ratio of 0.18 percent—it's low.

12b-1 Fee

A funny name for a fee? It's the government's rule number that allows funds to use their assets to pay for sales, marketing, and other fees—costs generated by the distribution of shares. It is an annual fee that is levied against the fund assets. Vanguard Index 500 has no 12b-1 fees.

Here's what we know about Vanguard's costs:

Front-end load = 0
Back-end load = 0
Expense ratio = 0.18 percent
12b-1 fee = 0
Total expenses: *0.18 percent*

In general, a fund with total expenses of less than 1.5 percent is considered a low-cost fund.

Your Take-Home Return

Let's go back to Vanguard's total returns. This number is not what investors make; we need to take into account the fund's expenses.

Vanguard Index 500 earned 19.8 percent in the past twelve months. Taking out the fund's expenses of 0.18 percent, we are left with 19.62 percent as our net return. In addition, we also like its risk level of "1," which is the same as the market.

It is a good fund to start with when you are building a portfolio of mutual funds.

Remember to look at the big picture when you're evaluating a fund. Don't merely be dazzled by returns, but check the expenses as well as the risks involved. The ideal investment is a fund with a low beta and a high return. It is your job as an informed investor to find funds that will offer you the highest rewards with the smallest risk.

Let's consider another fund: Flag Investors Communications Fund, Class A. The term "communications" in the name tells us that it's a sector fund and therefore we should expect higher volatility. The "A" means there is a front load.

GENERAL

NAV	39.87	NAV Change	0.43
Offer	41.75	Investment Category	SCIENCE & TECHNOLOGY
Total Net Assets ($millions)	1734.6	As of	06/30/99
Yield		As of	N/A
Volatility	7.21%	Beta	1.23

This fund's share price is $41.75 for buyers and $39.87 for sellers. The difference is the load. The beta is 1.23, or 23 percent higher than that of the S&P 500. Remember, the higher the beta, the more volatility we should expect.

PERFORMANCE AS OF 7/27/99

1 Week Performance	−2.60%	26 Week Performance	17.60%
1 Year Performance	65.20%	Year to Date Performance	21.30%
3 Year Performance	50.70%	3 Year Total Return	242.60%
5 Year Performance	35.30%	5 Year Total Return	353.90%
10 Year Performance	22.40%	10 Year Total Return	653.40%
Performance Since Inception	22.10%	Total Return Since Inception	2,132.30%
Quintile Rank—1 Year	3	Numeric Rank—1 Year	
Quintile Rank—3 Year	1	Numeric Rank—3 Year	2 of 32
Quintile Rank—5 Year	2	Numeric Rank—5 Year	6 of 22

Look at the performance of the fund. Make a note of where it falls in rank among all other sector funds, not the communications sector exclusively.

Now let's subtract the fees:

Fund Family		BT ALEX BROWN	
Manager Name		Behrens	
Manager Tenure	1984	Toll Free Phone	800-767-3524
Max Sales Charge	4.50%	12b-1 Fee	0.25%
Redemption Fee	0.00%	Min. Investment ($)	2,000
Fiscal Year End	12/31/97	Expense Ratio	1.11%
Income Divendends ($)	0.06	Capital Gains Divendends ($)	2.75
Ditribution Frequency	Quarterly		
Periodic Investment Plan?			
Systematic Withdrawal Plan?	Y		

Front-end load   =   4.5 percent
Back-end load   =   0
Expense ratio   =   1.11
12b-1 Fee   =   0.25
Total fees: 5.86 percent

We need to subtract the cost from the fund's return in the past twelve months to get the net return that went in each investor's pocket: 65.20 percent − 5.86 percent = 59.34 percent. Not bad.

Now you need to ask yourself this question: "Is it better to invest in a fund with a beta that is 23 percent higher than the market's but with a track record of these returns?" Only you can answer that question. Walk that tightrope between greed and fear. Can you handle it if the fund takes a dive? You decide.

How to Keep Track of Your Fund

Daily fund listings in your local newspaper offer a handy and easy way to keep up with your investments. Funds are listed alphabetically by fund family, followed by each mutual fund within that family.

Since fund share prices are updated only once a day at the market close, they do not fluctuate during the day the way stock prices do. You can calculate the value of your account by multiplying the last NAV published by the number of shares you own in the fund.

Review your fund's status periodically to make sure it isn't flagging in performance.

When your fund isn't performing as well as the current hot fund, don't be in a hurry to dump it and switch to the other. If you do this type of "fund bouncing," you'll end up selling low and buying high every time—a practice that will cost you a lot of money in the long run. If your fund is down but fundamentals are strong, the manager hasn't lost her mind, and the doldrums are mainly due to a hiccup in the market—it may be time to invest more money. The manager is probably trying to get back on track, so let him or her do their jobs and sit tight. Most people get impatient and sell at this crucial time, missing the great opportunity to buy more shares while the price is down. We should hunt for bargains among funds—unlike in stocks.

Your Conscience and Money

Money and heart can mix. You don't have to sacrifice your beliefs to make a buck. Today, there are plenty of these so-called green mutual funds that choose to invest exclusively in socially responsible companies—those that are conscientious about preserving the environment, paying fair wages, or supporting human rights. Green funds may also avoid companies that derive significant revenues from alcohol, tobacco, gambling, nuclear power, and weapons contracting. Green Century Equity, Domini Social Equity, and Pax World are among several socially conscious funds available today. Visit www.SocialFunds.com and www.Greenmoney.com for more information on green funds. But don't forget to screen any fund you find using the research tools we learned. After all, it's still an investment, not charity.

CHAPTER NINE

Starting an Investment Club

In one of my seminars, I passed around a hundred-dollar bill to the women in the room and asked each of them what it meant. That day, I heard more words for power, choice, and freedom than I ever had in my life. One woman held the bill in her hands and wept. She was struggling with her finances and realized that this green piece of paper was at the heart of her troubles. Indeed, many people struggle to save and invest. Baby boomers, who focused on their careers in the 1980s, are confronted with money realities today that may have been shoved aside in the past because they had so many expenses: buying a house, funding their kids' college tuition, and taking care of the needs of their aging parents. Sometimes, investing becomes a secondary priority for busy people. A question I often hear from successful women is this: "If I'm smart enough to run a company, why are my personal finances in such shambles?" They worked hard for their money all their lives and yet they have not experienced the empowerment that comes from seeing their money work for *them* for a change.

An investment club can help. This is a group of people who get together once a month to learn how to make money in stocks and mutual funds. The club meets for about two hours to talk about investment. Many people like joining clubs because they will not have to learn about investing by themselves and it takes up less of their time because members share the work.

To be part of an investment club, most likely you'll have to start one yourself. It is difficult to get into an existing club because the members tend to be friends and family. However, when someone leaves a club, the group might be willing to take you.

Forming a Club: Find People You Like

Start with a circle of friends and family. How many people should you invite? It depends on the size of the group you feel comfortable with. The National Association of Investors Corp., a nonprofit organization to which many investment clubs can belong, recommends about two dozen people. I have helped clubs with as few as eight members to as many as a hundred. I think fifteen is a good-sized club. You'll need enough members to build an investment pot with enough bite.

Make sure the people you invite will be able to stay in a room for two hours without getting into a brawl. Yes, personality and politics occur even in investment clubs. Believe it or not, innocent potluck parties can turn ugly.

For instance, one club of employees made the mistake of inviting the boss to join. She turned out to be, well, bossy. The worst part was that she was a terrible investor. However, since the members had to work for her, nobody contradicted her opinions. The club, which began on a profitable note, soon degenerated into a bickering mess. It was so stressful that club members started leaving. Finally, the group was dissolved. Ironically, the club's demise solved the problem. The boss left the group. Meanwhile, the employees formed another club—and didn't tell the boss about it.

Another club of kindhearted gals didn't expect that they would soon regret an act of charity. A friend of one of the members recently became a widow. Crestfallen, the woman was beside herself with grief and anxiety about the future. This club decided to adopt her—become her friends and coinvestors. The minute she joined, they knew they'd made a mistake. She was a dragon! She bossed people around and made everyone miserable. This club had been together for decades, but soon it was on the verge of dissolution. Nobody wanted to confront the widow; after all, she had just lost her husband. How could they be unkind? Thankfully, the woman's out-of-state daughter asked her mom to move in with her. The club was saved!

When you are inviting members to join, handle the invitation carefully as well. In my experience of helping form hundreds of clubs, I have found that the problem becomes more one of "No, you cannot join now, our club is closed," than of having to beg someone to participate. As soon as word gets out, people flock to join, even those you thought could care less about investing. I know two sisters who are not on speaking terms because one didn't invite the other to join her investment club.

The Investment-Club Starter Kit

When you form an investment club, you are creating a business entity called a general partnership. In the government's eyes, the club is a legal group. Although the club itself does not pay taxes, all profits passed on to members will be levied. That's right, the IRS wants its share from your little club that meets in the patio, and treats it the same way as it does Xerox Corp. To organize your club, ask for a starter kit from the NAIC. The kit will contain a guide to setting up clubs, the necessary legal forms, and other helpful material. For a small additional charge, they will also include bookkeeping software. To get the kit, one of the club's members has to join the NAIC and pay a small annual fee. For more information, call the organization at (877) ASK-NAIC or write to them at the National Association of Investors Corp., P.O. Box 220, Royal Oak, MI 48068. You also may check out their Web site at www.better-investing.org.

Set Up a Time and Place to Meet

Find the most convenient place and time to meet. It may be Saturday mornings at one of the members' homes, or it may be a weeknight at the conference room of the local chamber of commerce. Make sure the place is conducive to learning. Don't pick an area with many distractions, such as the center court of a mall. You don't want other people's ruckus to disturb your meeting. If anyone's going to make noise, it should be the club!

If possible, don't restrict the meeting's agenda strictly to business. Break the ice with an anecdote or two. Keep it light. Make it a social club as well, with picnics, parties, and potlucks. Such activities only build stronger relationships among members.

What to Do During Your First Meeting

* *Name your club.* Have a ball with this one. I've come across some creative examples: B.M.W. for Bull Market Women, Dough Makers, Well Stocked, Dow Dolls, and Stocking and Bonding. Let everyone come up with suggestions and take a vote. It can be a fun experience! When you name your club, you will feel like you have just given birth to someone dear. In a sense, you did. After all, the club will be an entity with its own Federal ID number, checking account, and investments.

* *Establish an investment goal.* Agree on an investment style. Are we conservative or aggressive investors? Do we want to marry our stocks—buy and hold—or date them—buy and sell? By agreeing on a style early on, the club will head off arguments later. Disagreements on how to invest have caused many clubs to disintegrate. Some women will want to know everything about an investment before they plunk their money down, while others are eager to buy and learn as they go along.

* *Choose an investment strategy.* Once you have agreed on your investment style, use the lessons we have learned in this book to pick your stocks and mutual funds. The NAIC has its own strategy, which is explained in a book they will send you along with the starter kit. While it is

a fine organization, I believe its investment style is hard to understand, tedious to learn, and boring. In addition, the NAIC uses fundamental analysis only. You need technical analysis too to increase your chances of making a profit.

• *Elect officers.* Pick responsible individuals. You might want to rotate the positions among the members every year so a handful of people won't be burdened forever. Here are the four officer positions:

  • President. She opens the meeting and serves as a moderator. She doesn't have to be a financial whiz, but she must know how to manage the club.
  • Vice-president. She has the least to do, but her role is no less important. She steps in when the president is otherwise unavailable. She also organizes social events and assigns tasks to other members.
  • Secretary. She takes notes during meetings and informs everyone when the next get-together will take place. Before every meeting, she reads the minutes from the last gathering. There is no need for her to make copies of the notes for every club member, so long as she keeps a record. I have heard minutes expressed in legalese as well as poems, songs, or jokes. The format doesn't matter. Again, keep it light, and enjoy yourselves.
  • Treasurer. This is the most important and critical job in the club. She collects, deposits, and keeps track of everyone's money. She's also responsible for giving each member a tally of the club's investments. If you want to be venerated, this is the job for you. Some clubs

have two people serving as treasurers. They might split the tasks or one can serve as the backup.

* *Attendance and participation.* A common cause of disagreement among club members is the unequal distribution of work. When you start a club, be prepared to have people who won't be pulling their weight. That's life. Don't get upset about it or set up strict rules that choke the other members. One club I know keeps a strict accounting of everyone's attendance and contribution; one toe out of line and it's good-bye club member! They're worse than the military. That said, it is still important to have rules. Some clubs impose a maximum number of absences before asking the member to leave. Do whatever works for everyone. The critical point is to agree on the rules before you start.

* *Voting.* You will have to vote on many things, but most often it will be to decide on an investment. Therefore, it's important to determine how many votes are needed for action. Some clubs require that a minimum number of members need to be present—a quorum—before they can take a vote. I don't recommend this. During the holidays, many members won't be able to attend meetings and the club will be unnecessarily tied down, unable to vote on buying and selling stocks. This is a better rule: If the club needs to vote, it doesn't matter how many people are at the meeting. If the majority of those present vote on a course of action, the decision will stand.

Show Me the Money

In the first three months of the club, I recommend that each member initially invests $10. Not only will it make the treasurer's job easier, an investment club is not the place for a big chunk of your life savings, your blood money. Instead, put in your bingo money. I don't want you to be afraid to lose your money when you're learning how to invest. Fear can interfere with your ability to make higher returns. The minute you are scared, you will retreat to your safety zone. You will feel the urge to pull your money out—and miss a learning opportunity. However, if you contribute only $10 a month, you will feel better about taking chances: "It's only $10. What do I care?"

After the third month, each member can contribute more money, but keep it in multiples of $10. Take pity on your treasurer, who has to track all the investments. You don't want her to tear her hair out, do you? A tip: Keep a basket at the door for members to put in their checks as they arrive.

Funds collected are divided into two pots: one for investments and the other for petty cash. Petty cash needs about $100 to pay the club's start-up expenses.

As for the investment pot, each $10 a member contributes entitles her to one unit. A hundred dollars will give you ten units. Initially, while the pot is growing, it will be easy to figure out how many units each member owns. But when the money is invested in stocks and it grows, calculating a member's ownership can be tricky. The NAIC kit will teach the treasurer how to do it manually, but I strongly recommend buying the bookkeeping software. It is easy to use and will figure out each member's portion of the pot quickly.

Each month, the investment money is totaled and divided by the number of units in the club. Each member will receive a statement showing the number of units she owns and the value of her holdings. For example, if Jane contributed $10 to the investment pot every month for half a year, she would have pitched in $60 and received six units in return. Let's say each of the other nine members of the club tossed in the same amount. After half a year the club's investment pot would contain $600. Each member has six units; the club has a total of sixty units.

If the club decided to invest in MiniMed, a maker of insulin pumps, for $57.50 a share, they would be able to buy ten shares and also pay the broker's $25 commission with their $600. If their investment grew to $70 a share in three months, their $600 pot is now worth $700 ($70 a share × ten shares). How much is due each member? Take $700 and divide by sixty units. The result is $11.67 per unit. Jane has six units, so her investment is worth $70.02. The MiniMed stock may be sold at a profit and the money is put back into the pool to await the next investment. Don't be in a hurry to take your money out. It's advisable to leave it in, because your primary purpose at the club is to learn about investing. With money already in the account, the club can act more quickly and efficiently on trades.

A member can put in more money, if she wishes. This is confidential; only the treasurer will know. However, set limits on deposits. You don't want to have someone investing $20 while the person next to her is depositing $200. This tends to give the $200 person a feeling of entitlement. Limit the deposit range to between $10 and $50 per month. Also, don't base your voting rights on members' deposits. One body equals one vote.

Trading Places

The club's money is deposited in a brokerage account. Choose a discount or online broker. It doesn't make sense to use a full-service broker because you want to learn to make investment decisions yourself. If you decide to open an account with a broker you know, don't feel pressured to do what he or she tells you. Your club will develop its own investment strategy that might go against what the broker believes. To prevent any unpleasantness, find another broker. The purpose of the club is to blaze a new trail, not follow the beaten path.

CHAPTER TEN

The Three-Drawer System: How to Allocate Your Investment Money

Doesn't the stock market sound exciting? I've had clients say they want to sell their houses or tap their home equity line to invest in stocks. Don't do it! Before you spend the last few dollars in your savings account on the market, take a minute to put everything in perspective.

Everyone should have three drawers in their financial planning system. Pretend that you're a recreational skier. You go skiing twice a year and the rest of the time you don't even look at the gear, much less remember where you stored it. If you have only one dresser, would you put your ski clothes in the top drawer? No, since you don't use them frequently.

If you're like me, you tuck away your Victoria's Secret—or is it Fruit Of The Loom?—underwear in the top drawer of your bedroom dresser because you can easily get to it. The bottom drawer holds your skiwear, which you only drag out once in a while. The middle drawer holds everything in between—T-shirts, casual blouses, shorts, and skirts.

Organize your investments according to this three-drawer system: Money that you'll need access to daily and quickly should be in the underwear drawer. This is the short-term and liquid file. Funds you don't need to touch until retirement belong in the bottom drawer. These are the long-term stuff that you cannot access before age fifty-nine and a half without a penalty. You don't pay taxes on them until the money is withdrawn. The middle drawer holds investments poised for growth.

The Top Drawer

Let's open the top drawer. What's in it? Money in your savings and checking accounts, certificates of deposit, money market accounts, and treasury bills. The top drawer is a revolving door, which money goes into and out of daily. These are funds you use to pay bills, buy food, and maintain your daily life. Okay, funds for a cruise-ship vacation *might* belong in this category; after all, it's an absolute necessity to provide a stash for rejuvenation, relaxation, and fun!

But you don't buy stocks with funds in this drawer. It's silly to sink every single penny you have here into the stock market. The minute you need to buy groceries, you will have to sell a share. You'll be miserable with an empty top drawer. Since you have invested the money you will need every day, you're going to panic and pull out of the market at the hint of a downturn. You're also going to sell at the wrong time because you're scared. This is how people get hurt. This drawer should hold enough money to pay bills plus a little cushion so you won't bounce any checks.

A certificate of deposit, or CD, also belongs here. It is a savings account that ties up your money for a specified period of time (thirty, sixty, ninety days, or longer) in exchange for a higher rate than regular passbook accounts. There are penalties if you withdraw your money before the end of your term. The interest earned on a CD is taxable at both state and federal levels. Initial deposits range from $1,000 and up.

Also in the top drawer are T-bills, or treasury bills. These are government IOUs. As such, they are safe since the U.S. government always pays back its loans. When you buy a T-bill, the government borrows money from you and pays interest. At the end of the T-bill's term, you will get your money back. You can buy a three-month, six-month, or one-year T-bills. The minimum for these securities used to be $10,000, but you can now open an account with as little as $1,000.

If you had a choice between investing in a CD or a T-bill, which one would be better? Let's say that you have a choice between a CD paying 5 percent interest and a T-bill giving you 3.8 percent. For every $1,000 you saved in a CD, you will earn $50. If you are in the 28 percent tax bracket, the money you will pocket from the CD will be about $36. Therefore, your real return on the CD is 3.6 percent ($36 divided by $1,000). The tax-free T-bill giving you 3.8 percent is a better deal.

You can buy T-bills from brokers, who will charge you a commission for opening an account, or directly from the U.S. Treasury Department. There are thirty-six Federal Reserve Banks throughout the U.S. that will serve you free of commission. In Los Angeles, the Federal Reserve Bank can be contacted at (213) 624-7398. The mailing address is P.O. Box 512077, Los Angeles, CA 90051-0077. In New York, call (212) 720-6619 or (212) 702-5823 (recording). Write them at FRB New York, P.O. Station,

New York, NY 10045-0001. Other Federal Reserve addresses can be found at www.publicdebt.treas.gov. You can open an account through the Internet and this site will guide you.

Money market mutual funds are another good place to park money you'll need to access quickly. Unlike a CD or a T-bill, it's not tied up for a period of time. It works like a stock or bond mutual fund, except that the managers buy treasury bills and short-term company loans called commercial paper, among other things. Although these aren't federally insured like your checking, savings, and CD accounts, they are generally considered safe. Money market mutual funds are available from most fund families and brokerage firms.

How much should you put in the top drawer? A good rule of thumb is at least six months' worth of living expenses just in case you lose your job, plus a bit extra for miscellaneous items. However, most of my clients complain about having too much money in their top drawer when it would be better allocated in the middle and bottom drawers. When you begin to invest your money, you will be tempted to move more of your top-drawer contents to the bottom. But try to maintain a balance. Don't tie up money in the market that doesn't belong there.

However, some of you may have so much money in the top drawer that you never have to worry about it running out. Don't take risks in the stock market. Why complicate your life? I've asked clients: "Why are you here? You don't need to worry about the market. You are wealthy." Even at the rates offered by savings, T-bills, and money market accounts, these clients would probably never run out of money. However, most of us are not in that category, so we have to invest our money well and wisely, balancing risk and reward.

What if your top drawer is empty? How can you have any

money to invest? You either need to make more money, or, here it comes . . . spend less. Nobody likes to hear that! But there's always something we can cut back on that won't make a big difference to our lifestyle. Be creative.

The Bottom Drawer

Don't put anything in this drawer you are planning to use before you are fifty-nine and a half years old. Here's the place for funds you'll keep in your retirement accounts: IRA, 401(k), 403(b), Keogh, and Sep-IRA. They may be invested in stocks, bonds, and other securities. You can't touch these investments without a 10 percent penalty from the government until the required age. However, while your money is growing, you don't pay taxes on it. You pay taxes when you withdraw the funds. These accounts are called *tax-deferred*. They are not tax-free.

Many financial planners will tell you that retirement accounts benefit investors because by the time you withdraw money from them, you will probably be in a lower tax bracket. You will be past your best earning years and probably retired. Forgive me for saying so, but why would anyone actually plan to be in a lower tax bracket by the time he or she retires? I hope to be in the same or a higher bracket by then. That means I am making just as much money as I am right now during my working years. I want to maintain or improve my standard of living, not lower it.

Even then, it makes sense to defer paying taxes on the money you have set aside for retirement and the profit it generates. Instead of letting a part of that money go to taxes, you can let it grow. Pay taxes later, when it's necessary.

What should you do with this money in the meantime? You

can transfer money between investments, with no tax consequences. These accounts, regardless of where they are, will remain
under the umbrella of a retirement account, exempt from taxes
until you withdraw the money. The transfers can be made directly
from one institution to another, which I recommend. If you close
the account and physically take receipt of the money, you have to
stick to a set of rules to ensure that you don't owe the government
any penalties or taxes.

By letting your institution transfer the money for you to another institution, you will bypass headaches from the government.
But there are other costs: The institutions themselves might
charge you for switching. Therefore, check with the investment
company before making any changes.

The Middle Drawer

I call this my greed drawer. Stocks, mutual funds, and some
types of annuities (for those past the age of fifty-nine and a half)
call this home. Notice that I have left out investments you may
have heard of such as limited partnerships and precious metals.
They may be interesting conversation pieces, but I've rarely found
people who have made money on them.

The difference between this drawer and the bottom one is ac-
cessibility; you can get to these investments without taking into
account any government rulings that regulate retirement accounts.
However, don't put anything in this drawer that you will need in
the next two to five years.

Use the money in this drawer to buy stocks, using fundamental
and technical analysis. Mutual funds have a place here too. Pick
among funds that hold stocks, bonds, or a combination of the two.

If you are over the age of fifty-nine and a half, you might want to consider an annuity as well.

An *annuity* is an investment account with an insurance company. It's not a life insurance policy. By buying an annuity, you and the insurer enter into a contract. You hand your money over to the insurance company, which will invest it for you. Sounds like a mutual fund? It works in a similar fashion. But it is tax-deferred, just like a retirement account.

Retirement? Shouldn't that be in the bottom drawer? Annuities fall into the middle drawer because investors have partial access to the money.

For example, you may be able to tap 10 percent of the account balance every year depending on the company issuing the annuity. However, you have to leave most of the money in the account for anywhere from one to fifteen years.

There are three kinds of annuities: fixed, variable, and index. In a *fixed annuity*, the insurance company guarantees that it won't pay you less than a certain amount of interest on your investment—such as 3 percent. Your principal is guaranteed not to fall in value as well. For safety of principal and a higher return on your money than a savings account, you sacrifice total access. However, fixed annuities have an advantage: They usually don't charge yearly maintenance fees.

In a *variable annuity*, the money is invested in mutual funds. Depending on the insurance company's policy, these funds could be part of a popular family that you can easily get information about or the insurer's own set of funds. If the insurance company issued these funds, you can get information about them only from the insurer itself.

The good news about variable annuities is that your returns can truly soar, depending on the funds you have chosen. But remember that they can also drop, since the insurance company does not guarantee a set interest rate. The only guarantee promised is that when you die, you will receive either all the original money you deposited in the account or the final account balance, whichever is greater.

This death protection plan does not come free. You pay a small percentage of your account's balance every year for it. There are other fees imposed on variable annuities in addition to those charged by the individual mutual funds. In addition, variable annuities also have early-withdrawal penalties.

A third kind of annuity is the *index annuity*. An index annuity is a fixed account whose returns are tied to the performance of the Standard & Poor's 500 Index. Here's the deal: If the index rises, investors will get a percentage of the gains. By contract, these percentages could never be less than half of the gain an index made. It could even go up to 100 percent.

The main difference between the index and other types of annuities is that if the index annuity drops, the original sum invested in the account will not decline in value. In some cases, the annuity guarantees an additional 3 percent. Again, this privilege comes with your willingness to have limited access to your account for perhaps several years.

Why invest in annuities? People in high tax brackets use them to shelter their money. You can put only so much money in other retirement accounts because they have maximum contributions per year. The well-heeled folks who want to keep their money away from Uncle Sam a little bit longer buy annuities.

How to Pick an Annuity

- Get a no-load annuity with neither maintenance nor account fees.

- Find out if the insurance company compounds the interest so you will end up with more money.

- Do they lock in your gains? They should.

- How strong is the insurance company? You don't want it to fail. Look up companies that rate insurers by their financial health. A. M. Best, Duff & Phelps, Standard & Poor's, and Moody's all report on them. Their reports on insurance companies are available in the public library or online. I personally favor A. M. Best because they don't charge the insurer to rate them. Others do. Can you see the conflict of interest? How can you trust a rating if you know the insurance company paid the agency who issued the report? Insurers are rated A+, A, A−, B+, B, B−, and so on. We want only an A rating for our insurance companies.

- If you are in an annuity you don't like, you can switch to another one. But find out if there is a penalty. Sometimes you might want to take the penalty if the profits from another annuity will well outweigh the costs.

- Always ask your investment advisor, "Is there anything else I should know that I have not asked you about?" You want to know everything and you might just be surprised at what you hear.

How to Stuff Your Drawers

Let's take a look at our three drawers and their contents:

Checking Account,
Savings Account,
Money market Fund, CD,
or T-Bill

Mutual Funds, Stocks
Annuities
(if over 59½)

Retirement Accounts such
as IRA's, KEOGH's,
401(k), 403(b), etc.
Equity in your home,
Annuities

How do you allocate your money?

Start from the top drawer. Any wages, commissions, and income you receive should go there every month. The money left over at the end of the month, *before* you deposit your next paycheck, should be moved to the middle drawer. But don't get overzealous. Remember to leave room for bills that sneak up on us once or twice a year, like car insurance and taxes. You may also want to consider adding some money to your bottom drawer. But remember to kiss this money good-bye until retirement.

If you don't have any money to move from the first to the second drawer, take a hard look at your spending habits. You have to make a choice: Do you want to invest or not? If so, you have to make some changes to your spending.

As you make money in your middle drawer, you may want to move some to the bottom drawer as well. What you decide depends on your tax situation.

The Reverse Drawers

After you retire, how will you use the three drawers? Start from the middle and bottom, and move to your top drawer—daily living expenses. Figure out how much money you will need to live on every month and arrange to have that amount withdrawn from the middle and bottom drawers. Put that in your top drawer.

But how much will we have by then? It depends on how much you have saved and what return you have been earning.

The Savings Plan

We all have different ideas about how much money we will need when we retire. It depends on your necessities and lifestyle. But let's hypothesize for a minute. If you invest $100 a month, how much will you have at retirement? It depends on several factors. Look at the table on the next page.

$1,200 per year at varying rates compounded annually
(end of year values)

	5th YEAR	10th YEAR	15th YEAR	20th YEAR	25th YEAR	30th YEAR	35th YEAR	40th YEAR
3%	6,182	14,169	22,988	33,211	45,063	58,803	74,731	93,195
5%	6,962	15,848	27,188	41,662	60,135	83,713	113,803	152,208
10%	8,059	21,037	41,940	75,602	129,818	217,131	357,752	584,222
15%	9,304	28,018	65,660	141,372	293,654	599,948	1,216,015	2,455,144
20%	10,716	37,380	103,730	268,831	679,652	1,701,909	4,245,610	10,575,154

According to our table, if you invest $1,200 a year, or $100 monthly, in an investment paying you an average of 5 percent a year, you should have $6,962 after five years. In fifteen years, your account balance would be $27,188. In thirty-five years—$113,803.

How much richer would you be if you earned an average return of 15 percent? Your account would grow to $9,304 in five years, $65,660 in fifteen years, and $1.2 million in thirty-five years.

Imagine if you saved and invested twice the amount per year. Your account balance would be double what you see on the table. For example, you would have $282,744 after twenty years if you're earning an average return of 15 percent. If you can save only $50 a month, cut the table's figures in half. Therefore, a 10 percent investment will yield $20,970 after fifteen years.

But how long will this money last? It depends on how much you withdraw from the account every year and what return it is earning. Look at the next table.

Percentage of original principal withdrawn per year	Total Return per year on balance of principal						
	3%	4%	5%	6%	7%	8%	9%
	Principal will last . . .						
4%	46 yr						
5	30	41 yr					
6	23	28	36 yr				
7	18	21	25	33 yr			
8	15	17	20	23	30		
9	13	14	16	18	22	28 yr	
10	12	13	14	15	17	20	26 yr

If you have $300,000 in your retirement account, how long can you live on it? To calculate whether you will have enough, first determine what percentage of your retirement money you want to live on per year. Then figure out what portion it represents of your retirement funds. For example, if you want to withdraw $18,000 a year from a $300,000 account, you would be taking out 6 percent of your principal every year ($18,000 divided by $300,000 and multiplied by 100). Look up 6 percent in the left column. Put a finger there. Next, find out how much interest you are earning on the $300,000 account. Assuming it is 4 percent, look up the percentage in the top row. Crisscross both numbers and you come to twenty-eight years. Your money will last twenty-eight years.

If you want a more comfortable retirement, you will have to withdraw more money. Let's say you want to draw 10 percent every year, or $30,000. You want to travel, take up hobbies, and enjoy life more fully. How can you afford to withdraw that much money? You can if you have been earning a 9 percent average annual return. Your capital will last almost as long as the 4 percent account—twenty-six years. To live better, you didn't have to save more money; you earned a higher return. The 4 percent account will enable you to survive, but the 9 percent will let you live.

Do you see how critically important it is to invest in the stock market? Only stocks can give you an average annual return of 10 percent a year. So be smart about money. It may make the difference between walks in the public park for leisure and strolls along the beaches of the Bahamas.

A Final Word

We've had a heart-to-heart talk about making money. I hope I have sparked some excitement in you about investing. If I have accomplished that, then writing this book was worth it. My goal was to teach you, the novice investor, the tools you need to start planning for a secure financial future.

The tools you have learned are a stepping-stone to more complex investment strategies. Let me tell you something that probably no other investment book will even dare say: There isn't one foolproof investment strategy. If there were only one way to stock market riches, why would there be a proliferation of investment theories and books? Once you become an experienced investor, you will develop your own strategy that is based on what you've read and observed. You will blend different investment styles to form your own.

The Big Rocks

After you delve into the world of finance, remember to put everything in perspective. Remember the big rocks—and I don't mean diamonds, although there's nothing wrong with having them too. The big rocks are what's truly important in life. Let me share a story with you.

One day, an expert in time management was speaking to a group of business students. To drive home a point, he used an illustration the students will never forget. As he stood in front of the group of high-powered overachievers, he said, "Okay. Time for a quiz."

He pulled out a one-gallon, widemouthed mason jar and set it on a table in front of him. Then he produced a dozen fist-sized rocks and carefully placed them, one at a time, into the jar. When the jar was filled to the top and no more rocks would fit inside, he asked, "Is this jar full?"

Everyone in the class said yes. He said, "Really?" He reached under the table and pulled out a bucket of gravel. He dumped some gravel in and shook the jar, causing pieces of gravel to work themselves down into the spaces between the big rocks. Then he asked the group once more, "Is the jar full?"

By this time the class had caught onto him. "Probably not," one of them answered. "Good!" he replied. He reached under the table and brought out a bucket of sand. He started dumping the sand in. It flowed into all the spaces left between the rocks and the gravel. Once more he asked the question, "Is this jar full?" "No!" the class shouted. Once again he said, "Good!"

He grabbed a pitcher of water and began to pour it in until the jar was filled to the brim. Then he looked up at the class and asked, "What's the point of this exercise?" One eager beaver raised his hand and said, "The point is, no matter how full your schedule is, if you try really hard, you can always fit more things into it!"

"No," the speaker said. "That's not the point. The truth this illustration teaches us is this: If you don't put the big rocks in first, you'll never get them in at all."

What are the "big rocks" in your life? Time with your loved ones? Your faith, your education, your dreams? A worthy cause teaching or mentoring others? Remember to put these big rocks in first or you'll never get them in at all. Don't compromise on your principles or beliefs.

I strongly believe that when you do what you love doing most, the money will follow.

The Journey Continues

I feel like a momma bird pushing her babies out of the nest. I've tried to give you all the information you need to spread your wings and take flight into the world of investing. But like every mother, I want you to know that I will still be here if you need me. I will be waiting for you at http://www.JulieStav.com.

At this site you will find ways to review what you have learned. I will keep you updated on the changes that constantly take place in the market, help you appraise the market atmosphere, discuss stocks that meet our standards, and help you choose the best time to invest in these promising companies. I can help you establish and run successful and fun investment clubs with people who share your interests and investing style.

Come visit and feel free to email me your comments, concerns and suggestions, so that we can get to know each other better and through our experiences help those who follow.